▶ **Britain's Last Religious Revival?**

DOI: 10.1057/9781137512536.0001

Histories of the Sacred and the Secular 1700–2000

General Editor: **Professor David Nash, Oxford Brookes University, UK**

Editorial Board:

Professor Callum Brown, Glasgow University, UK

Professor William Gibson, Oxford Brookes University, UK

Dr Carole Cusack, Sydney University, Australia

Professor Beverley Clack, Oxford Brookes University, UK

Dr Bert Gasenbeek, Humanist University, Utrecht, Netherlands

Professor Paul Harvey, University of Colorado at Colorado Springs, USA

This series reflects the awakened and expanding profile of the history of religion within the academy in recent years. It intends publishing exciting new and high quality work on the history of religion and belief since 1700 and will encourage the production of interdisciplinary proposals and the use of innovative methodologies. The series will also welcome book proposals on the history of Atheism, Secularism, Humanism and unbelief/secularity and to encourage research agendas in this area alongside those in religious belief. The series will be happy to reflect the work of new scholars entering the field as well as the work of established scholars. The series welcomes proposals covering subjects in Britain, Europe, the United States and Oceana.

Titles include:

John Wolffe (*editor*)
IRISH RELIGIOUS CONFLICT IN COMPARATIVE PERSPECTIVE
Catholics, Protestants and Muslims

Clive D. Field
BRITAIN'S LAST RELIGIOUS REVIVAL?
Quantifying Belonging, Behaving, and Believing in the Long 1950s

Forthcoming titles:

Jane Platt
THE ANGLICAN PARISH MAGAZINE 1859–1929

Histories of the Sacred and the Secular 1700–2000
Series Standing Order ISBN 978–1–137–32800–7 (Hardback)
(*outside North America only*)

You can receive future titles in this series as they are published by placing a standing order. Please contact your bookseller or, in case of difficulty, write to us at the address below with your name and address, the title of the series and the ISBN quoted above.

Customer Services Department, Macmillan Distribution Ltd, Houndmills, Basingstoke, Hampshire RG21 6XS, England

DOI: 10.1057/9781137512536.0001

palgrave▸pivot

Britain's Last Religious Revival? Quantifying Belonging, Behaving, and Believing in the Long 1950s

Clive D. Field
University of Birmingham, United Kingdom

palgrave
macmillan

DOI: 10.1057/9781137512536.0001

First published 2015 by
PALGRAVE MACMILLAN

Palgrave Macmillan in the UK is an imprint of Macmillan Publishers Limited, registered in England, company number 785998, of Houndmills, Basingstoke, Hampshire RG21 6XS.

Palgrave Macmillan in the US is a division of St Martin's Press LLC, 175 Fifth Avenue, New York, NY 10010.

Palgrave Macmillan is the global academic imprint of the above companies and has companies and representatives throughout the world.

Palgrave® and Macmillan® are registered trademarks in the United States, the United Kingdom, Europe and other countries.

ISBN: 978-1-137-51254-3   EPUB
ISBN: 978-1-137-51253-6   PDF
ISBN: 978-1-137-51252-9   Hardback

A catalogue record for this book is available from the British Library.

A catalog record for this book is available from the Library of Congress.

www.palgrave.com/pivot

DOI: 10.1057/9781137512536

Contents

DOI: 10.1057/9781137512536.0001

List of Tables

DOI: 10.1057/9781137512536.0002

Preface

Secularization has been a defining characteristic of the historiography of religion in modern Britain since the 1960s. The term (and the associated notion of a secular society) has a much earlier derivation, of course, but first became fashionable in scholarly discourse through the work of sociologists such as Bryan Wilson whose *Religion in Secular Society: A Sociological Comment* (London: C.A. Watts, 1966) remains influential. Latterly, the mantle of secularization has passed to Steve Bruce, who continues to advocate it vigorously, most recently in his *Secularization: In Defence of an Unfashionable Theory* (Oxford: Oxford University Press, 2011).

At its simplest, secularization is no more than a descriptive shorthand for the declining social significance of religion. However, when cast in the form of a 'thesis', 'theory', or 'paradigm', and imputed with teleological, causative, explanatory, and predictive properties, it has become a much more contested concept and is by no means universally accepted as a 'master narrative' for religious change. It has been hotly (and, one has to say, not always productively) debated by historians and sociologists, sometimes obscuring the empirical evidence base along the way. A key component of the debate has surrounded the chronology of secularization and particularly whether it has been a progressive and gradual phenomenon or a revolutionary and sudden one.

Callum Brown has been the most persuasive proponent of the revolutionary school, viewing the 1960s as the critical secularization decade, in Britain and elsewhere, in terms both of the decline of organized religion (specifically Christianity) and the disappearance of a dominant Christian culture and values. Other leading scholars are also agreed on the existence of a 'religious crisis' in the 1960s. Additionally, Brown has suggested that this dramatic development was preceded in Britain during the late 1940s and early 1950s by a return to piety and exceptional church growth. This claim has been met with more scepticism by his peers, but it has still not been subjected to rigorous empirical validation or refutation. What will be termed here the 'long 1950s' remain a neglected period in the social history of modern British religion, notwithstanding significant writing about its more ecclesiastical and biographical aspects.

This short monograph brings quantitative data and insights to bear on British religion in the 1950s, examining it through the three principal lenses – belonging, behaving, and believing (the content of, respectively, Chapters 2, 3, and 4) – which are increasingly used to characterize the study of popular religion. Although statistics by no means tell the whole story, and qualitative sources remain important in documenting and understanding religious behaviour, Brown's claims for the immediate post-war period are of such a nature that they should be capable of quantitative scrutiny. In recent years, research culminating in the *British Religion in Numbers* (BRIN) project has helped to uncover a wider range of source material for this era than has previously been identified or utilized. These sources are briefly described in Chapter 1, which also outlines the historiographical context in more detail. Chapter 5 attempts a balance sheet of the measurable changes in the British religious landscape during the 1950s.

DOI: 10.1057/9781137512536.0003

Acknowledgements

The author has incurred a number of debts over the years, especially to those who have facilitated access to unpublished material. In particular, thanks are due to Bob Wybrow of the now defunct Social Surveys (Gallup Poll) Ltd for opening up early Gallup files; to the late David Glass who supplied extracts from his then (and still) unpublished book on the Third Londoner Survey (the current whereabouts of the original being unknown); and to Tony Spencer of the Pastoral Research Centre Trust for copying or loaning reports from the Trust's Newman Collection.

A small grant from the British Academy some years ago assisted with initial research into opinion polls on religion. Further sources were identified through the *British Religion in Numbers* project, which was supported for three years by the Arts and Humanities Research Council and the Economic and Social Research Council.

Ben Clements of the University of Leicester kindly commented on a first draft of the book and provided analyses of several datasets distributed by the United Kingdom Data Archive.

The Mass-Observation Archive (M-OA) is a charitable trust in the care of the University of Sussex and is made available to scholars courtesy of The Trustees of the Mass-Observation Archive. The collection is housed at The Keep, Brighton, as part of the university's special collections, and that repository's shelf marks for M-OA documents have been cited in the endnotes for this book. However, all such documents have actually been consulted in *Mass-Observation Online*, a sub-set of M-OA published in facsimile by Adam Matthew Digital.

List of Abbreviations

Gallup Social Surveys (Gallup Poll), formerly British
        Institute of Public Opinion
GIPOP   G.H. Gallup, ed., *The Gallup International Public
        Opinion Polls: Great Britain, 1937–1975* (1976)
M-O   Mass-Observation
M-OA   Mass-Observation Archive, The Keep, Brighton
NDS   Newman Demographic Survey
UKDA   United Kingdom Data Archive

▶

DOI: 10.1057/9781137512536.0005

1
Introduction

Abstract: *This introductory chapter summarizes the recent historiography of secularization in modern Britain, including Callum Brown's claims for religious resurgence during the late 1940s and early 1950s. The gloomier assessment of contemporaries about the religious health of the nation is noted, as is the relative ineffectiveness of mass evangelism during the 'long 1950s', notably Billy Graham's crusades. The sources to be used in the statistical evaluation of Brown's claims are introduced, some collected by the Churches, some by opinion poll and other social research agencies, some by individual academics. Any methodological or interpretative challenges posed by these sources are briefly mentioned. Finally, the precise chronological parameters of the study are set (1945–63) and compared with those used by Brown and other scholars.*

Keywords: 1950s; Callum Brown; historiography; religious revival; secularization; statistical sources

Field, Clive D. *Britain's Last Religious Revival? Quantifying Belonging, Behaving, and Believing in the Long 1950s.* Basingstoke: Palgrave Macmillan, 2015. DOI: 10.1057/9781137512536.0006.

Historiography

Few observers would dispute that modern British society has become less religious over time, but fundamental disagreements exist among historians and sociologists concerning the exact chronology, nature, and causation of such a process of secularization.[1] In particular, as it affected Christianity, there are divergent views about whether it has been a gradualist or revolutionary phenomenon, originating either with industrialization and urbanization or only in more contemporary times. Much recent scholarly attention has focused on the pace of religious change during the 1960s, in Britain and other western nations, with Callum Brown advancing a strong case for regarding these years as 'the secularisation decade', when a 'discourse revolution' took place, 'a remarkably sudden and culturally violent event' which spelled the end for 'discursive Christianity' and sent 'organised Christianity on a downward spiral to the margins of social significance'.[2] Hugh McLeod, whom Brown regards as a member of the gradualist school of secularization, has offered a more nuanced interpretation of the 'religious crisis' of the 1960s, although even he still considers these years as 'marking a rupture as profound as that brought about by the Reformation', emphasizing especially the weakening of religious socialization of youth.[3] Other present-day writers have also seen the 1960s as a turning point in Britain's religious history.[4]

Brown's thesis has an additional twist to it. Not only were the 1960s an era of revolutionary secularization, but they were immediately preceded by 'something of a religious boom' and a 'return to piety' during the late 1940s and 1950s, at least until 1956, in some cases even to 1959. Although he is by no means the first scholar to make such a suggestion,[5] Brown pursues the argument with great conviction. This epoch, he continues, was characterized by 'one of the most concerted periods of church growth since the middle of the nineteenth century' (elsewhere he suggests since the eighteenth century), with 'surges of ... church membership, Sunday school enrolment, [and] accompanied by immense popularity for evangelical "revivalist" crusades'. Of special significance was the 'extraordinary' level of religious activity among the young, who 'became more than unusually enthusiastic patrons of churches, church coffee bars and Billy Graham's crusade'. These years likewise witnessed 'one of the high points of British Christian culture, surpassed only by that of the Edwardian period', with 'a vigorous reassertion of "traditional" values', epitomized by an intensification of moral and sexual conservatism and a

DOI: 10.1057/9781137512536.0006

reassertion of the role of women as wives and mothers. Indeed, through 'this conservative family context', religion became more gendered and dependent on underpinning by a reaffirmed female 'piety' and 'puritanical notions of female respectability'. Overall, 'people's lives in the 1950s were very acutely affected by genuflection to religious symbols, authority and activities... Religion mattered and mattered deeply in British society as a whole in the 1950s.' 'Discursive Christianity' – 'the vigour of its hegemonic Christian culture' – was a power in the land and 'religious conformity was at its height'.[6] Such claims are advanced by Brown particularly enthusiastically in relation to Scotland.[7]

Brown's reading of the late 1940s and 1950s has not gone unchallenged. McLeod accepts the continuation of a Christian culture but contends that 'the post-war revival was... more modest and less widely spread than in the United States', certainly as regards England and Wales, and proposes an alternative 'double-sided' relationship between the 1950s and 1960s, rather than seeing them as 'polar opposites'.[8] Matthew Grimley reports a mixed picture post-war, Nonconformity continuing to decline but Anglicanism rallying, while providentialist ideas and language decayed and the association between religion and national character weakened.[9] Simon Green views the 1950s as a decade of 'false hopes' so far as institutional religion was concerned, dismisses its 'so-called "religious revival"' as 'a lamentable failure', and concludes that 'Britain had ceased to be a Christian country by 1960'.[10] In a similar vein, Nigel Yates deems the revival 'very fragile' and notes that the religious leadership of the 1950s 'had already prepared for ways in which the churches might come to terms with the growing secularization of society and the questioning of traditional moral values'. In general, he adds,

> the two decades between 1950 and 1970 need to be seen as a single period in which considerable moral, religious and social change took place in Britain, but on the whole much more slowly and often less dramatically than some have believed... In every case the events of the 1960s have had the ground laid for them, to a very large extent, in the 1950s.[11]

From his Black Country perspective, Richard Sykes also contests, or at least heavily qualifies, Brown's interpretation of the late 1940s and early 1950s, preferring to see the Second World War as a more important religious watershed.[12] However, other evidence – quantitative at the national level (analysed by Clive Field)[13] and qualitative at the local level (Stephen Parker)[14] – suggests that wartime religion was relatively

DOI: 10.1057/9781137512536.0006

resilient, and that the Second World War was not a particularly major short-term milestone in Britain's secularization history.[15] Steve Bruce and Tony Glendinning, by contrast, think the war did leave an enduring secularizing legacy by disrupting community ties and family formation and, in the long run, negatively impacting the transmission of faith from one generation to the next. They further discount Brown's notion of post-war church growth: 'Some indices of church involvement increase after 1945 but not all do, none does by much, and none come close to their Victorian or Edwardian peaks when expressed as percentages of the available population.'[16] In this they echo the opinions of earlier religious historians such as Alan Gilbert ('the recovery which followed in the late 1940s and early 1950s was minimal even in comparison with the short-lived upturn after the First World War'),[17] or Ian Machin ('the Protestant Churches preserved reasonable stability in the post-war years up to 1960, but did not achieve collectively a revival of numbers and influence to the levels of three or four decades before').[18]

Generalist historians of post-war British society have also struggled to see how it was especially religious. Thus, for Peter Hennessy 'mid-century Britain was still a Christian country only in a vague attitudinal sense, belief generally being more a residual husk than a kernel of conviction'[19]; and for David Kynaston 'it is hard to see how Britain in the 1950s can, in any meaningful sense, be called a Christian society'.[20] Perhaps the latest secondary source which comes closest to validating Brown's approach is Ian Jones's study of Birmingham, which perceives 'the crisis of church participation in the 1960s' to have been preceded by 'a genuine (if short-lived) religious renewal in the early to mid-1950s', including 'the temporary revival of churchgoing', albeit one which was 'strongly (if not exclusively) associated with children and young adults'.[21]

But it is not just recent historians who have been sceptical about Brown's case. Many contemporaries also expressed a lack of confidence in the health of the post-war religious commonwealth. There was a powerful sense that the nation needed to be respiritualized and the bulwarks reinforced against the godless communism of an emergent Cold War with its implicit threat – possibly an even greater threat than Nazism – to the values of Christian civilization.[22] Christianity in danger was a recurring theme in the literature of the day, with quite a lot of loose talk about 'paganism' and 'heathenism'. The religious ignorance of the young was exposed, to widespread consternation, in surveys of cadets[23] and naval conscripts.[24] Seebohm Rowntree, the eminent Quaker, tried to bring

DOI: 10.1057/9781137512536.0006

some social scientific rigour to the matter, convinced that 'we are ... living on the spiritual capital of the past'.[25] Few observers were upbeat about the prospects for organized religion. As Stephens Spinks lamented in 1952: 'in the years that followed the war, ministers of many denominations who had hoped for a "Return to Religion" experienced periods of great depression ... there was no marked renewal of church life'.[26]

It was not for want of trying. For the perceived need to recharge the religious batteries had led to a fresh commitment to evangelism after the Second World War, embodied in the Anglican report *Towards the Conversion of England*.[27] First published in June 1945, and reprinted seven times by January 1946, it found some practical expression in local missions, most notably in London in 1949.[28] Among the Free Churches, the Methodists had their Christian Commando Campaigns (1943–47)[29] and the Order of Christian Witness, established by Donald Soper in 1946[30]; the Baptists had the Baptist Advance of 1949–51; the Congregationalists the Congregational Forward Movement of 1950–53[31]; and the Churches of Christ a Crusade of Christian Witness of 1950–53. Evangelistic activities in Scotland were spearheaded by D.P. Thomson and Tom Allan of the Church of Scotland before broadening out into the pan-Protestant Tell Scotland Movement.[32] Even the Catholics were not left behind, the Catholic Missionary Society organizing a general mission to recover lapsed Catholics in 1949–50, and Patrick Peyton conducting crusades in 1951–52.[33]

Most celebrated of all, of course, were the missions of the American Billy Graham, initially in 1946–49, then in London in 1954, Glasgow and London in 1955, and Manchester, Glasgow, and Belfast in 1961. Graham's crusades certainly attracted large audiences (2,046,000 in London in 1954 and 1,185,000 in Glasgow in 1955), but the proportion who came forward for counselling was low (around 2 per cent in each case), and these 'converts' were disproportionately women, young people, and those already connected with a church.[34] Three-quarters of his Manchester enquirers in 1961 were also already churchgoers, while four-fifths of the genuine 'outsiders' had dropped away from the Christian life within a few years.[35] The pre-Graham initiatives likewise appear to have had limited impact, to judge by Scottish experience.[36] Unsurprisingly, therefore, Brown does not attempt to build his case for a 'return to piety' mainly, if much at all, on the outcomes of such evangelism; 'the success in numbers attending', he concedes, 'did not translate into significant church growth'.[37]

DOI: 10.1057/9781137512536.0006

Sources

In this short book we shall seek to test Brown's arguments for 'something of a religious boom' occurring during the late 1940s and early 1950s by recourse to other, and particularly quantitative, evidence. This is in full recognition that Brown's case rests on qualitative as well as quantitative sources, and that his claims about the enduring, if not intensifying, cultural significance of Christianity and about 'religious austerity' derive from autobiography and oral history. The statistics will be drawn from a range of measures. Brown has been critical of some historical accounts of (gradualist) secularization in Britain for being over-dependent on churchgoing data,[38] so we will be deploying, to a greater or lesser extent, each of the four indicators which Brown urges for a balanced assessment of religious change: church attendance; church membership and adherence; religious or nonreligious beliefs; and identification with a religion or none.[39] They are rearranged here under the broader headings of religious belonging, religious behaving, and religious believing, so as to map on to the wider literature about secularization. Our principal focus will be on studies of the adult population, with somewhat less attention paid to investigations of children and adolescents.[40]

The contemporary statistics were collected by three main agencies. The Churches had mostly counted their flocks at least annually since the late nineteenth century, and their key series have been conveniently collated in *Churches and Churchgoers*.[41] But they often remained suspicious of sociological approaches and techniques. Indeed, according to the industrial missioner E.R. Wickham, in his ground-breaking study of the religious life of Sheffield, 'the churches do not ask embarrassing sociological questions', adding: 'To reject the new instruments or to restrict their use to the "social sciences" would be blasphemy whereby God is yet further banished to the shrinking area of the inexplicable and the arbitrary.'[42] The principal exception to this aversion was the Roman Catholic Church in England and Wales, which was briefly (1953–64) served by the Newman Demographic Survey (hereafter NDS).[43] Among Protestant bodies, the Methodist Church was one of the first to embrace the potential of sociology, establishing a sociological sub-committee of its Church Membership Committee in 1961.[44] In the Church of England, the first Director of Religious Sociology was Leslie Harman, in the Diocese of Southwark in 1963.[45] More ecumenical was the Christian Economic

DOI: 10.1057/9781137512536.0006

and Social Research Foundation, established in 1953, but the bulk of its work concerned alcohol, not religion *per se*.[46]

Secondly, there were some academic studies. However, they were not especially numerous, the sociology of religion, *qua* discipline, being in a very embryonic condition in Britain in the 1950s, as several literature reviews revealed.[47] This state of affairs was reflected in the preponderance of American evidence in Michael Argyle's celebrated work of synthesis in 1958, written from the perspective of social psychology.[48] Not until 1967 was a dedicated sociological overview of English religion published, by David Martin,[49] indicative of the fact that the subject was finally taking off in British universities, albeit the volume was deficient in statistics, as the author later conceded.[50] It was followed the following year by the first issue of *A Sociological Yearbook of Religion in Britain*.[51]

Finally, opinion poll and other social research organizations were then emerging as a real force, even if their techniques were relatively primitive by modern social scientific standards. The latter was perhaps still true of the two best-known agencies, the British Institute of Public Opinion (later Social Surveys, Gallup Poll)[52] and Mass-Observation (hereafter M-O),[53] both of which commenced operations in 1937, with other companies starting up after the war.[54] Besides generic methodological issues, polls pose a number of other challenges when applied to religion, which need to be borne in mind.[55] An example is the relatively high proportion of 'don't knows' for many religious questions, exemplified in the elderly gentleman who, when asked whether he believed in life after death, 'looked quizzically at the interviewer and said: "I don't know Miss, but I'll damn soon find out." '[56] Relevant polls have been identified from *British Religion in Numbers*, whose source database provides descriptive and bibliographical information for each survey.[57] References in the text have accordingly been confined to noting fieldwork date, agency, and the principal publication(s) only. In the case of Gallup, the most active of the polling companies, there is a well-indexed compendium of topline results for most published surveys.[58]

It should be remembered that, although not released until 1947 (with a second impression in 1948), *Puzzled People* by M-O, one of the most celebrated polls, was actually based on fieldwork in the London borough of Hammersmith between October 1944 and January 1945 and thus did not strictly reflect post-war attitudes.[59] It is likewise important not to be beguiled by all the tables in Geoffrey Gorer's *Exploring English Character*, which has been so routinely mined by historians and sociologists

DOI: 10.1057/9781137512536.0006

(including Brown). This book's data largely derived from a self-selecting sample of readers of *The People*, a tabloid Sunday newspaper, in January 1951, and they did not constitute a representative national cross-section, with a particularly strong bias toward the under-35s and men.[60]

As for retrospective sources, caution also needs to be exercised in drawing upon the work of Peter Brierley, the doyen of current (post-1970) church statistics, who has additionally attempted some quantification of the British religious scene going back to 1900. Although he has used *Churches and Churchgoers* as the basis of these calculations, he has seemingly filled in the many gaps, not by primary research on historical sources, but by back-projection techniques. Some of his tabulations, while looking complete and authoritative, are actually rather misleading. As an example, we may note his quinquennial statistics of religious community in the United Kingdom, which appear to suggest that the irreligious constituted 19 per cent of the population in 1945 rising to 23 per cent in 1965, whereas the real proportion of 'nones' was significantly lower. Brierley also exaggerates the size of the non-Christian constituency for this period.[61]

Defining the decade

A preliminary word should be said about chronological focus. The 'long 1950s' is here defined in its most inclusive sense, spanning 1945–63. This is quite deliberate, so that, where appropriate, we can compare and contrast the period before 1956 or so, which coincided with Brown's suggested 'age of piety', and the years immediately afterwards, 1956–63, when, according to Brown, religious decline started to emerge in advance of more cataclysmic change setting in from 1963. For, he contends, it was 'really quite suddenly in 1963' that 'something very profound ruptured the character of the nation and its people',[62] making that year a logical terminus for this monograph. It should be noted that Brown himself deploys the notion of the 'long 1960s' (sometimes delimited as 1956–73 and sometimes as 1957–75) alongside one of the 'short 1960s' (1963–70). McLeod, in his book on the religious crisis of the 1960s, similarly utilizes the concept of the 'long 1960s' (1958–74) but sub-divides it into the 'early' (1958–62), 'mid' (1963–66), and 'late' (1967–74) 1960s. Both scholars thus align themselves with Arthur Marwick who, in his more general history of the decade, defined the 'long 1960s' as subsuming 1958–74.[63]

DOI: 10.1057/9781137512536.0006

Notes

1   The term 'secularization' is used throughout in a purely descriptive sense, to denote the process whereby religion has declined in institutional, personal, and socio-cultural significance. This book does not set out to engage with the *theory* of secularization as debated in the sociological literature.

2   His writings on the 1960s are extensive, and the following is a necessarily selective list: C.G. Brown, 'The Secularisation Decade: What the 1960s Have Done to the Study of Religious History', in H. McLeod and W. Ustorf, eds, *The Decline of Christendom in Western Europe, 1750–2000* (Cambridge: Cambridge University Press, 2003), pp. 29–46; idem, *Religion and Society in Twentieth-Century Britain* (Harlow: Pearson, 2006), pp. 224–77; idem, *The Death of Christian Britain: Understanding Secularisation, 1800–2000* (2nd edn, London: Routledge, 2009), pp. 170–92; idem, 'What Was the Religious Crisis of the 1960s?' *Journal of Religious History*, 34 (2010), pp. 468–79; idem, 'Gendering Secularisation: Locating Women in the Transformation of British Christianity in the 1960s', in I. Katznelson and G. Stedman Jones, eds, *Religion and the Political Imagination* (Cambridge: Cambridge University Press, 2010), pp. 275–94; idem, 'Women and Religion in Britain: The Autobiographical View of the Fifties and Sixties', in C.G. Brown and M. Snape, eds, *Secularisation in the Christian World: Essays in Honour of Hugh McLeod* (Farnham: Ashgate, 2010), pp. 159–73; idem, 'Sex, Religion, and the Single Woman, *c.* 1950–75: The Importance of a "Short" Sexual Revolution to the English Religious Crisis of the Sixties', *Twentieth Century British History*, 22 (2011), pp. 189–215; idem, *Religion and the Demographic Revolution: Women and Secularisation in Canada, Ireland, UK, and USA since the 1960s* (Woodbridge: Boydell Press, 2012); idem, 'Gender, Christianity, and the Rise of No Religion: The Heritage of the Sixties in Britain', in N. Christie and M. Gauvreau, eds, *The Sixties and Beyond: Dechristianization in North America and Western Europe, 1945–2000* (Toronto: University of Toronto Press, 2013), pp. 39–59; and idem, 'Unfettering Religion: Women and the Family Chain in the Late Twentieth Century', in J. Doran, C. Methuen, and A. Walsham, eds, *Religion and the Household* (*Studies in Church History*, 50, Woodbridge: Boydell Press, 2014), pp. 469–91.

3   H. McLeod, 'The Sixties: Writing the Religious History of a Critical Decade', *Kirchliche Zeitgeschichte*, 14 (2001), pp. 36–48; idem, 'The Religious Crisis of the 1960s', *Journal of Modern European History*, 3 (2005), pp. 205–30; idem, 'Why Were the 1960s So Religiously Explosive?' *Nederlands Theologisch Tijdschrift*, 60 (2006), pp. 109–30; idem, 'The Crisis of Christianity in the West: Entering a Post-Christian Era?' in H. McLeod, ed., *The Cambridge History of Christianity, Volume 9: World Christianities, c. 1914–c. 2000* (Cambridge: Cambridge University Press, 2006), pp. 323–47; idem, *The Religious Crisis of the 1960s* (Oxford: Oxford University Press, 2007); idem, 'The 1960s', in Katznelson

and Jones, eds, *Religion and the Political Imagination*, pp. 254–74; and idem, 'European Religion in the 1960s', in S. Hermle, C. Lepp, and H. Oelke, eds, *Umbrüche: der deutsche Protestantismus und die sozialen Bewegungen in den 1960er und 70er Jahren* (2nd edn, Göttingen: Vandenhoeck & Ruprecht, 2012), pp. 35–50.

4   Recent contributions include: G. Parsons, 'How the Times They Were a-Changing: Exploring the Context of Religious Transformation in Britain in the 1960s', in J.R. Wolffe, ed., *Religion in History: Conflict, Conversion, and Coexistence* (Manchester: Open University Press, 2004), pp. 161–89; S. Wright, *The Sounds of the Sixties and the Church* (Guildford: Grosvenor House, 2008); N. Yates, *Love Now, Pay Later? Sex and Religion in the Fifties and Sixties* (London: SPCK, 2010); S.J.D. Green, *The Passing of Protestant England: Secularisation and Social Change, c. 1920–1960* (Cambridge: Cambridge University Press, 2011), especially pp. 273–302; J. Maiden and P. Webster, 'Parliament, the Church of England, and the Last Gasp of Political Protestantism, 1963–4', *Parliamentary History*, 32 (2013), pp. 361–77; R. Freathy and S.G. Parker, 'Secularists, Humanists, and Religious Education: Religious Crisis and Curriculum Change in England, 1963–1975', *History of Education*, 42 (2013), pp. 222–56; and S. Brewitt-Taylor, 'The Invention of a "Secular Society"? Christianity and the Sudden Appearance of Secularization Discourses in the British National Media, 1961–4', *Twentieth Century British History*, 24 (2013), pp. 327–50.

5   For instance, Adrian Hastings had written of 'the modest religious revival' which characterized 1945–60 in his *A History of English Christianity, 1920–1985* (London: Collins, 1986), pp. 443–4, 461, 464–5.

6   Brown, *Religion and Society*, pp. 26, 177–223; idem, *Death of Christian Britain*, pp. 5–7, 11, 14, 170–5, 187–9, 212–15; idem, ' "The Unholy Mrs Knight" and the BBC: Secular Humanism and the Threat to the "Christian Nation", *c.* 1945–60', *English Historical Review*, 127 (2012), pp. 345–76, at pp. 347–9, 356; idem, *Religion and the Demographic Revolution*, pp. 47–53; idem and G. Lynch, 'Cultural Perspectives', in L. Woodhead and R. Catto, eds, *Religion and Change in Modern Britain* (London: Routledge, 2012), pp. 329–51, at pp. 331–3.

7   C.G. Brown, 'Religion and Secularisation', in T. Dickson and J.H. Treble, eds, *People and Society in Scotland, III, 1914–1990* (Edinburgh: John Donald, 1992), pp. 52–3; idem, *The People in the Pews: Religion and Society in Scotland since 1780* (Glasgow: Economic and Social History Society of Scotland, 1993), pp. 44–5; idem, *Religion and Society in Scotland since 1707* (Edinburgh: Edinburgh University Press, 1997), pp. 1, 158–9, 163.

8   McLeod, *Religious Crisis of the 1960s*, pp. 10, 37–9, 65.

9   M. Grimley, 'The Religion of Englishness: Puritanism, Providentialism, and "National Character", 1918–1945', *Journal of British Studies*, 46 (2007), pp. 884–906, at pp. 887, 905–6.

DOI: 10.1057/9781137512536.0006

10 S.J.D. Green, 'Was There an English Religious Revival in the 1950s?' *Journal of the United Reformed Church History Society*, 7 (2006), pp. 517–38; and idem, *Passing of Protestant England*, pp. 242–72, 313.

11 Yates, *Love Now, Pay Later?* pp. 151–4.

12 R.P.M. Sykes, 'Popular Religion in Dudley and the Gornals, c. 1914–1965' (PhD thesis, University of Wolverhampton, 1999), pp. 299–352; and idem, 'Popular Religion in Decline: A Study from the Black Country', *Journal of Ecclesiastical History*, 56 (2005), pp. 287–307, at pp. 291–3.

13 C.D. Field, '*Puzzled People* Revisited: Religious Believing and Belonging in Wartime Britain, 1939–45', *Twentieth Century British History*, 19 (2008), pp. 446–79.

14 S.G. Parker, *Faith on the Home Front: Aspects of Church Life and Popular Religion in Birmingham, 1939–1945* (Oxford: Peter Lang, 2005).

15 The religious impact of the First World War was likewise less cataclysmic than is often imagined; C.D. Field, 'Keeping the Spiritual Home Fires Burning: Religious Belonging in Britain during the First World War', *War & Society*, 33 (2014), pp. 244–68.

16 S. Bruce and T. Glendinning, 'When was Secularization? Dating the Decline of the British Churches and Locating its Cause', *British Journal of Sociology*, 61 (2010), pp. 107–26, at pp. 115, 120–3.

17 A.D. Gilbert, *The Making of Post-Christian Britain: A History of the Secularization of Modern Society* (London: Longman, 1980), p. 77.

18 G.I.T. Machin, *Churches and Social Issues in Twentieth-Century Britain* (Oxford: Clarendon Press, 1998), p. 172.

19 P. Hennessy, *Never Again: Britain, 1945–51* (London: Jonathan Cape, 1992), p. 436.

20 D. Kynaston, *Family Britain, 1951–57* (London: Bloomsbury, 2009), p. 535.

21 I. Jones, *The Local Church and Generational Change in Birmingham, 1945–2000* (Woodbridge: Boydell Press, 2012), pp. 55–69, 84–93, 148–67.

22 O. Chadwick, *The Christian Church in the Cold War* (London: Allen Lane, 1992); D. Kirby, *Church, State, and Propaganda: The Archbishop of York and International Relations – A Political Study of Cyril Foster Garbett, 1942–1955* (Hull: University of Hull Press, 1999); and idem, ed., *Religion and the Cold War* (Basingstoke: Palgrave Macmillan, 2003). Kirby has also written several articles on religion and the Cold War.

23 B.G. Sandhurst [pseudonym of C.H. Green], *How Heathen Is Britain?* (London: Collins, 1946, rev. edn, 1948).

24 G. Layton, 'Religion', *The Navy*, 52 (1947), pp. 147–8.

25 B.S. Rowntree and G.R. Lavers, *English Life and Leisure: A Social Study* (London: Longmans, Green, 1951), pp. 339–74; M. Freeman, ' "Britain's Spiritual Life: How Can It Be Deepened?" Seebohm Rowntree, Russell Lavers, and the "Crisis of Belief", ca. 1946–54', *Journal of Religious History*,

DOI: 10.1057/9781137512536.0006

29 (2005), pp. 25–42; S.J.D. Green, 'Social Science and the Discovery of a "Post-Protestant People"', *Northern History*, 45 (2008), pp. 87–109; idem, *Passing of Protestant England*, pp. 180–208; and idem, 'A People beyond the Book? Seebohm Rowntree, the Decline of Popular Biblicism, and the Fate of Protestant England, *c.* 1900–50', in S. Mandelbrote and M. Ledger-Lomas, eds, *Dissent and the Bible in Britain, c. 1650–1950* (Oxford: Oxford University Press, 2013), pp. 256–76. Rowntree died in 1954 before completion of his proposed major work on 'The Spiritual Life of the Nation'.

26 G.S. Spinks, *Religion in Britain since 1900* (London: Andrew Dakers, 1952), p. 224.

27 Commission on Evangelism of the Church Assembly, *Towards the Conversion of England* (London: Press and Publications Board of the Church Assembly, 1945).

28 By way of illustration, the parish mission at Immanuel Church, Streatham Common between 27 March and 2 April 1949 was appraised by M-O in FR 3121, 'Report on a Mission' (1949), Brighton, The Keep, M-O Archive [hereafter M-OA], 1/1/14/5/3.

29 C.A. Roberts, ed., *These Christian Commando Campaigns: An Interpretation* (London: Epworth Press, 1945); D. Gowland and S. Roebuck, *Never Call Retreat: A Biography of Bill Gowland* (London: Chester House, 1990), pp. 54–72.

30 D. Thompson, *Donald Soper: A Biography* (Nutfield: Denholm House Press, 1971), pp. 102–8; B. Frost, *Goodwill on Fire: Donald Soper's Life and Mission* (London: Hodder and Stoughton, 1996), pp. 180–4.

31 A. Argent, *The Transformation of Congregationalism, 1900–2000* (Nottingham: Congregational Federation, 2013), pp. 436–8.

32 J. Highet, *The Scottish Churches: A Review of Their State 400 Years after the Reformation* (London: Skeffington, 1960), pp. 89–123; F.D. Bardgett, 'The Tell Scotland Movement: Failure and Success', *Records of the Scottish Church History Society*, 38 (2008), pp. 105–50.

33 J. Hagerty, 'The Conversion of England: John Carmel Heenan and the Catholic Missionary Society, 1947–1951', *Recusant History*, 31 (2013), pp. 461–81; A. Harris and M. Spence, ' "Disturbing the Complacency of Religion"? The Evangelical Crusades of Dr Billy Graham and Father Patrick Peyton in Britain, 1951–54', *Twentieth Century British History*, 18 (2007), pp. 481–513.

34 F. Colquhoun, *Harringay Story: The Official Record of the Billy Graham Greater London Crusade, 1954* (London: Hodder and Stoughton, 1955); T. Allan, ed., *Crusade in Scotland: Billy Graham* (London: Pickering & Inglis, 1955); S. Herron, 'What's Left of Harringay?' *British Weekly*, 10 February 1955; D.J. Jeremy, *Capitalists and Christians: Business Leaders and the Churches in Britain, 1900–1960* (Oxford: Clarendon Press, 1990), pp. 397–410; I.M. Randall, 'Conservative Constructionist: The Early Influence of Billy Graham in

DOI: 10.1057/9781137512536.0006

Britain', *Evangelical Quarterly*, 67 (1995), pp. 309–33; idem, 'Billy Graham, Evangelism, and Fundamentalism', in D.W. Bebbington and D.C. Jones, eds, *Evangelicalism and Fundamentalism in the United Kingdom during the Twentieth Century* (Oxford: Oxford University Press, 2013), pp. 173–91; Harris and Spence, ' "Disturbing the Complacency of Religion"?'

35 Anon, 'Does it Last?' *Crusade*, 12 (1966), pp. 15–17.

36 Highet, *Scottish Churches*, pp. 89–123; J. Highet, 'The Churches', in J. Cunnison and J.B.S. Gilfillan, eds, *The Third Statistical Account of Scotland: Glasgow* (Glasgow: Collins, 1958), pp. 734–42.

37 Brown, *Religion and Society*, pp. 195, 201; idem, *Death of Christian Britain*, pp. 173–4; idem, *Religion and Society in Scotland*, pp. 163–4, 198.

38 Brown, *Religion and the Demographic Revolution*, pp. 39, 43, 88.

39 Ibid., p. 72.

40 For a guide to the research literature on children and adolescents for this period, see C.D. Field, 'Non-Recurrent Christian Data', in W.F. Maunder, ed., *Religion* (Reviews of United Kingdom Statistical Sources, 20, Oxford: Pergamon Press, 1987), pp. 259–67. There is an overview of studies among higher education students in J.B. Brothers, 'Religion in the British Universities: The Findings of Some Recent Surveys', *Archives de Sociologie des Religions*, 9 (1964), pp. 71–82.

41 R. Currie, A.D. Gilbert, and L. Horsley, *Churches and Churchgoers: Patterns of Church Growth in the British Isles since 1700* (Oxford: Clarendon Press, 1977). The appendix of data tables is also available in Excel format at http://www.brin.ac.uk/figures/#ChurchesandChurchgoers.

42 E.R. Wickham, *Church and People in an Industrial City* (London: Lutterworth Press, 1957), pp. 14–15, 217; J. Morris, 'Church and People Thirty-Three Years On: A Historical Critique', *Theology*, 94 (1991), pp. 92–101. There had been five impressions of Wickham's book by 1964, with a paperback edition launched in 1969.

43 A.E.C.W. Spencer, 'The Newman Demographic Survey, 1953–62: Nine Years of Progress', *Wiseman Review*, 236 (1962), pp. 139–54; idem, 'The Newman Demographic Survey, 1953–1964: Reflection on the Birth, Life, and Death of a Catholic Institute for Socio-Religious Research', *Social Compass*, 11 (1964), pp. 31–40; idem, 'The Newman Demographic Survey', in *A Use of Gifts: The Newman Association, 1942–1992* (London: Newman Association, 1992), pp. 34–7; idem, ed., *Annotated Bibliography of Newman Demographic Survey Reports & Papers, 1954–1964* (Taunton: Russell-Spencer, 2006); and C.D. Field, *Religious Statistics in Great Britain: An Historical Introduction* (Manchester: Institute for Social Change, University of Manchester, 2010), pp. 82–6.

44 D. Wollen, 'Sociology and the Church Membership Committee', *London Quarterly and Holborn Review*, 188 (1963), pp. 26–33.

45 *Sunday Times*, 10 February 1963.

DOI: 10.1057/9781137512536.0006

46   Archives at London Metropolitan Archives, LMA/4006. The Foundation ceased in 1985.

47   N. Birnbaum, 'La sociologie de la religion en Grande-Bretagne', *Archives de Sociologie des Religions*, 1 (1956), pp. 3–16; C.K. Ward, 'Sociological Research in the Sphere of Religion in Great Britain', *Sociologia Religiosa*, 3 (1959), pp. 79–94; N. Birnbaum, 'Soziologie der Kirchengemeinde in Grossbritannien', in D. Goldschmidt, F. Greiner, and H. Schelsky, eds, *Soziologie der Kirchengemeinde* (Stuttgart: Ferdinand Enke, 1960), pp. 49–65; J.A. Banks, 'The Sociology of Religion in England', *Sociologische Gids*, 10 (1963), pp. 45–50; and J.B. Brothers, 'Recent Developments in the Sociology of Religion in England and Wales', *Social Compass*, 11 (1964), pp. 13–19. For Scotland, see J. Highet, 'A Review of Scottish Socio-Religious Literature', *Social Compass*, 11 (1964), pp. 21–4; and idem, 'Trend Report on the Sociology of Religion in Scotland', *Social Compass*, 13 (1966), pp. 343–8.

48   M. Argyle, *Religious Behaviour* (London: Routledge & Kegan Paul, 1958).

49   D.A. Martin, *A Sociology of English Religion* (London: SCM Press, 1967).

50   D.A. Martin, *The Education of David Martin: The Making of an Unlikely Sociologist* (London: SPCK, 2013), p. 131.

51   (8 vols, London: SCM Press, 1968–75). The first two volumes were edited by Martin, the third by Martin and M. Hill, and the final five by Hill alone.

52   M. Roodhouse, ' "Fish-and-Chip Intelligence": Henry Durant and the British Institute of Public Opinion, 1936-63', *Twentieth Century British History*, 24 (2013), pp. 224–48.

53   J. Hinton, *The Mass Observers: A History, 1937–1949* (Oxford: Oxford University Press, 2013); and, for a contemporary critique, M.A. Abrams, *Social Surveys and Social Action* (London: William Heinemann, 1951), pp. 105–13.

54   N. Moon, *Opinion Polls: History, Theory, and Practice* (Manchester: Manchester University Press, 1999), pp. 14–23.

55   C.D. Field, 'Repurposing Religious Surveys', in L. Woodhead, ed., *How to Research Religion: Putting Methods into Practice* (Oxford: Oxford University Press, forthcoming).

56   H. Durant and W. Gregory, *Behind the Gallup Poll, with a Detailed Analysis of the 1951 General Election* ([London]: News Chronicle, [1951]), p. 27.

57   http://www.brin.ac.uk/sources/. A thematic checklist of religion-related opinion polls to 1982 also appears in Field, 'Non-Recurrent Christian Data', pp. 327–442.

58   G.H. Gallup, ed., *The Gallup International Public Opinion Polls: Great Britain, 1937–1975* [hereafter *GIPOP*] (2 vols, New York: Random House, 1976). This was drawn upon by R.J. Wybrow, *Britain Speaks Out, 1937–87: A Social History as Seen through the Gallup Data* (Basingstoke: Macmillan, 1989).

59   M-O, *Puzzled People: A Study in Popular Attitudes to Religion, Ethics, Progress, and Politics in a London Borough* (London: Victor Gollancz, 1947). Raw

material from this study is preserved at M-OA, 1/2/47/13/A-K, 1/2/47/14/A-E. There is also a folder of press notices and sales figures at M-OA, 1/2/47/3E (sales seem to have been around 3,400 copies). Field, '*Puzzled People* Revisited', draws heavily on the book's findings.

60   G.E.S. Gorer, *Exploring English Character* (London: Cresset Press, 1955). Raw material from this study is preserved at Brighton, The Keep, Geoffrey Gorer Archive, SxMs52.

61   P.W. Brierley, ed., *UK Christian Handbook, Religious Trends, No. 2, 2000/01 Millennium Edition* (London: Christian Research, 1999), p. 2.7. Other versions of this table (with slight variations) appear in P.W. Brierley, *Religion in Britain, 1900 to 2000* (London: Christian Research, 1998), p. 2; and idem, 'Religion', in A.H. Halsey and J. Webb, eds, *Twentieth-Century British Social Trends* (Basingstoke: Macmillan, 2000), pp. 652–3.

62   Brown, *Death of Christian Britain*, p. 1. The significance of 1963 is explained at greater length in idem, *Religion and Society*, pp. 224–5, where Brown also sees 1967 as another turning point.

63   A. Marwick, *The Sixties: Cultural Revolution in Britain, France, Italy, and the United States, c. 1958–c. 1974* (Oxford: Oxford University Press, 1998).

DOI: 10.1057/9781137512536.0006

2
Belonging

Abstract: *This chapter considers the two main dimensions of religious belonging: religious affiliation and church membership. In the absence of census data for this period, religious affiliation statistics can be derived only from contemporary and retrospective sample surveys. These are summarized, with breaks by key demographic variables. Church membership data are more plentiful, but there are many gaps and many problems of comparability. Actual and estimated church membership statistics are provided for all denominations and faiths (including organized irreligion), noting short-term movements within the decade, where appropriate. These include Sunday school data in the case of Protestant Churches, thereby ensuring a level playing field with the Roman Catholic Church, which defined its membership in terms of its baptised population.*

Keywords: church membership; religious affiliation; religious belonging; sample surveys; Sunday schools

Field, Clive D. *Britain's Last Religious Revival? Quantifying Belonging, Behaving, and Believing in the Long 1950s.* Basingstoke: Palgrave Macmillan, 2015.
DOI: 10.1057/9781137512536.0007.

DOI: 10.1057/9781137512536.0007

Affiliation

We commence our investigation of Brown's claims about religious vitality during the 1950s with an analysis of religious belonging, which embraces the concepts of religious affiliation and religious membership. In many foreign countries and parts of the British Empire/Commonwealth a question about religious affiliation was a standard component of the national census of population from the later nineteenth century, including in Ireland from 1861 (and, following partition, in Northern Ireland from 1926). But it was never a feature of the British census at this time (it was eventually introduced in 2001), initially on account of the diametrically opposed positions on the matter taken up by Anglicans and Nonconformists, tempers only cooling with the achievement of Welsh disestablishment.[1] The Church Assembly passed a resolution in 1945 in favour of religious affiliation being included in the 1951 census,[2] but the request seems to have been ignored by Government and the issue was not raised in Parliament. In 1960, John Parker, Dagenham's Labour MP, moved to insert religion when the draft Order in Council for the 1961 census was debated in the House of Commons, following his earlier correspondence with the Home Office on the subject. Parker's rationale was public expenditure on church-run schools and the need for its evidential basis. Responding for Government, Niall Macpherson (Joint Under-Secretary of State for Scotland) dismissed the idea, commenting that 'there is considerable resistance towards giving this kind of information and we are advised that the questions would probably be widely resented and in consequence we would not be likely to get the sort of truthful answers which we seek to obtain in the census.'[3] The decision disappointed Tony Spencer of the NDS, who continued to argue the case for a religious census.[4] However, academics did not rush to agree with him. Indeed, John Highet, perhaps the most noted sociologist of religion during the long 1950s, dismissed censuses of religious affiliation in 1962 as 'singularly worthless.'[5]

In the absence of information from the census, sample surveys are the principal source for religious affiliation. They divide into those which were conducted at the time and those undertaken after the long 1950s but which asked about religion of upbringing during the 1950s. Mostly they were representative of the adult population of Britain, which is our focus here, but it should be noted that a few local surveys were also undertaken, perhaps the most interesting (not least since it attempted to

DOI: 10.1057/9781137512536.0007

reconcile its returns with church records and because it was replicated subsequently) being in Banbury in 1950.[6]

Only a selection of the contemporaneous national polling data on religious affiliation can be recovered, as summarized in Table 2.1. The results are not wholly consistent, arising from sampling error, variations in question-wording,[7] and differences in the way specific denominations were assigned to the religious groupings. In general, however, it can be said that one-half to three-fifths of Britons professed to be Anglicans,[8] one-fifth affiliated as Free Church or Presbyterian (mostly Church of Scotland in the latter case), one-tenth were Catholic, and less than one-tenth had no religion. The number of professing 'nones' was somewhat inflated by Gallup's early practice of including non-respondents in this category. In terms of the polls, the big growth in

TABLE 2.1   *Religious affiliation of adult population, Great Britain, 1946–63 (percentages across)*

Date	Agency	N	Church of England	Free Church/ Presbyterian	Roman Catholic	Other religion	No religion
7–8/1946	Gallup	3,239	45	27	11	6	11
9/1947	Odhams Press	3,019	54	22	9	7	8
1947–49	Gallup	?7,000	51	23	11	6	9
9/1948	Daily Express	?	60	16	8	11	5
1/1950	Gallup	2,000	51	23	11	6	9
5/1952 (E&W)	Gallup	4,948	61	16	10	6	7
12/1954	Gallup	1,859	53	22	8	7	7
2/1957	Gallup	2,261	55	22	9	5	9
3/1960	Gallup	1,000	56	24	10	6	4
11/1960	Gallup	1,150	62	18	10	5	5
11/1962	Gallup	1,000	61	19	10	5	5
12/1962	Gallup	1,000	58	21	11	4	6
5–8/1963	BMRB	2,009	65	23	9	1	3
8–12/1963	Gallup	21,495	61	19	10	4	6

Sources: 7–8/1946 = 'British Institute of Public Opinion (Gallup) Polls, 1938–1946', dataset at UKDA [distributor], SN 3331 – analysis by B. Clements; 9/1947 = *News Review*, 6 November 1947; 9/1948 = *Daily Express*, 20 September 1948; 2/1957 = *News Chronicle*, 16 April 1957, G.H. Gallup, ed., *The Gallup International Public Opinion Polls: Great Britain, 1937–1975* (2 vols, New York: Random House, 1976), i., p. 404; 5–8/1963 = 'Political Change in Britain, 1963–1970', dataset at UKDA [distributor], SN 44 – analysis by B. Clements; 8–12/1963 = J. Brothers, *Religious Institutions* (London: Longman, 1971), p. 12; all other dates = unpublished tables in author's possession.

DOI: 10.1057/9781137512536.0007

'nones' seems to have occurred, not during the 1960s, as one might have expected from Brown's work, but in the late 1970s and 1980s.[9] Crude comparisons can be drawn between the position in *c.* 1963 (mainly based on Gallup's aggregated sample of 21,500 interviews) and that in *c.* 1914 and *c.* 1939 (Table 2.2). This reveals some recovery in Anglican allegiance since 1939, seemingly at the expense of a reduction in the Free Church and Presbyterian constituency, together with an increase in 'nones'.

Polls enable religious affiliation to be disaggregated by sundry demographic variables, and examples are provided in Tables 2.3 and 2.4 based on pooling, respectively, two Gallup surveys in 1946 and four in 1947–49. In regional terms, Anglicans were especially thick on the ground in Southern England and the Midlands, the Free Churches in Wales, the Church of Scotland in Scotland, Catholics in Northern England and Scotland, with 'nones' slightly over-represented among Southerners. The main gender differentials were a tendency for Roman Catholics to be disproportionately female and a marked predominance of men for those professing no religion. 'Nones' were most likely to be found among people in their twenties,[10] while Free Church affiliates were showing signs of ageing and concentration in the over-fifties. Judged by perceived income, Anglicans partly lived up to their reputation of being moderately wealthy and Roman Catholics of being relatively poor. Occupationally, 57 per cent of 'nones' were manual workers on weekly wages (compared with a national average of 42 per cent) and just 13 per cent were housewives (who were most numerous in the Church of Scotland and Roman Catholic Church). Church of Scotland followers were especially located

TABLE 2.2   *Estimated religious affiliation of adult population, Great Britain, c. 1914, c. 1939, and c. 1963 (percentages down)*

	1914	1939	1963
Church of England	64	55	61
Roman Catholic	6	11	10
Free Church/Presbyterian	28	29	22
Non-Christian	1	1	1
No religion	1	4	6

Sources: 1914 from C.D. Field, ' "The Faith Society"? Quantifying Religious Belonging in Edwardian Britain, 1901–1914', *Journal of Religious History*, 37 (2013), p. 62; 1939 from C.D. Field, 'Gradualist or Revolutionary Secularization? A Case Study of Religious Belonging in Inter-War Britain, 1918–1939', *Church History and Religious Culture*, 93 (2013), p. 91; and 1963 modified from J.B. Brothers, *Religious Institutions* (London: Longman, 1971), p. 12.

DOI: 10.1057/9781137512536.0007

TABLE 2.3   *Religious affiliation by demographics, Great Britain, 1946 (percentages down)*

	All	Church of England	Church of Scotland	Free Church	Roman Catholic	Other	None
N	3,115	1,406	256	585	342	198	328
Gender							
Men	51	50	51	49	45	50	72
Women	49	50	49	51	55	50	28
Age (years)							
21–29	14	14	14	11	15	16	20
30–49	48	48	50	48	50	43	49
50+	37	37	36	41	35	41	31
Income							
Average+	7	8	8	6	6	12	5
Average	24	24	28	24	17	26	23
Average-	69	67	64	70	77	62	72
Occupation							
Professional/executive	9	8	8	9	8	12	10
Clerical	9	10	13	8	5	7	6
Proprietor/farmer	5	4	2	6	5	9	5
Weekly wages: industry	17	15	10	17	20	13	25
Weekly wages: agriculture	2	2	6	3	1	2	4
Weekly wages: other	23	23	22	21	21	23	28
Housewives	27	28	33	29	32	25	13
Retired/unoccupied	9	10	5	8	8	9	9

Source: Aggregate of July and August 1946 surveys from 'British Institute of Public Opinion (Gallup) Polls, 1938–1946', dataset at UKDA [distributor], SN 3331 – analysis by B. Clements.

in the clerical and agricultural sectors but were under-represented in industry.

The picture is complicated somewhat by denominational switching, 13 per cent telling Gallup in February 1957 that they had formerly belonged to a different denomination than at interview.[11] This phenomenon was further explored through religious life histories in Rawmarsh and Scunthorpe in 1954–56, revealing that, at the time of interview, 39 per cent followed a different denomination than the one with which they had been associated until the age of 16. However, the sample was fairly small and it was restricted to active church members, not extending to the general population.[12] A major cause of such switching was the tendency of wives to adopt their husbands' denomination on marriage, illustrated in a Welsh community study of the late 1940s.[13] Certainly, contemporary surveys suggested that the norm was for husbands and wives to profess the same religion.[14]

The British Social Attitudes (BSA) Surveys are probably the most interesting of the retrospective sources.[15] One standard question has been

DOI: 10.1057/9781137512536.0007

TABLE 2.4   *Religious affiliation by demographics, Great Britain, 1947–49 (percentages across)*

	Church of England	Church of Scotland	Free Church	Roman Catholic	Other	None
All	51	8	15	11	6	9
Gender						
Men	50	8	14	11	6	11
Women	51	8	16	12	7	6
Age (years)						
21–29	50	7	12	13	6	12
30–49	51	8	15	12	6	8
50–64	53	8	16	10	6	7
65+	48	9	19	12	6	6
Income						
Higher	55	9	13	9	8	6
Middle	53	8	12	10	7	10
Lower	51	8	15	12	5	9
Very poor	48	6	17	14	6	9
Region						
Southern	58	2	13	9	7	11
Midlands	63	0	18	8	5	6
Northern	53	2	16	15	6	8
Wales	43	1	32	6	10	8
Scotland	6	61	1	18	5	9

Source: Unpublished table in author's possession, aggregating four British Institute of Public Opinion (Gallup) Polls with a total sample of *c.* 7,000.

about religion of upbringing. Here we have aggregated the responses for adults aged 45–54 for the nine surveys between 1991 and 2000 (there was none in 1992), this being the cohort best approximating to the generation growing up in the late 1940s and 1950s. Of 4,740 respondents, 58 per cent reported that they had been brought up as Anglicans, 13 per cent as Catholics, 21 per cent as other Christians, 3 per cent as non-Christians, and 5 per cent as without religion. In two of these years, 1991 and 1998, interviewees in the same cohort were also asked about their parents' religion when they had been a child. A similar pattern of replies emerged, 6 per cent of parents having no religion (9 per cent of fathers and 4 per cent of mothers), with 51 per cent being Anglican, 13 per cent Catholic, 24 per cent other Christian, and 2 per cent non-Christian. A somewhat higher rate of non-affiliation (13 per cent) was reported in the Medical Research Council National Survey of Health and Development, which interviewed in 1972 (when aged 26) 3,743 persons born during one

DOI: 10.1057/9781137512536.0007

week in March 1946, 57 per cent reporting their upbringing as Anglican, 9 per cent as Catholic, and 21 per cent as other Christian.[16]

However, parents were not necessarily strongly attached to their religion, nor did they go to excessive lengths to pass it on to their children. This was demonstrated in the 1986 BSA in which 71 per cent of the 542 individuals growing up in the 1940s and 1950s recollected that their parents had made little if any attempt to persuade their children to share their own religious beliefs; the 28 per cent who had tried very or quite hard to do so were most likely to be found in Catholic families. A similar picture emerges from other surveys. Thus, in the 1974 and 1979 British Election Studies, 32 per cent of the 1,349 respondents in the 1940s and 1950s generation had been brought up as practising members of some denomination, whereas 27 per cent had not been and 42 per cent only to some extent.[17] In the 1990 European Values Survey, 64 per cent of 478 members of the same generation recalled being brought up religiously at home and 36 per cent not.[18]

Membership – general

Self-identified religious affiliation is obviously a fairly passive indicator, involving no real effort on the part of the believer and being purely a matter of declaration. Church membership, by contrast, is a more active measure of religious belonging, necessitating some form of registration by a religious denomination. Unfortunately, there is no common criterion of church membership, definition being a matter for each religious body, making it problematical to produce comparative national estimates. Notwithstanding, some attempts to do so were made, both during the long 1950s and retrospectively for the 1950s. Among contemporary efforts, John Highet's estimates for Scotland (Table 2.5) are most useful, with church membership approaching three-fifths of the adult (over 20) population in 1947 (56.2 per cent),[19] 1951 (57.8 per cent), 1957 (59.5 per cent), 1959 (59.0 per cent), 1964 (58.5 per cent), and 1966 (58.5 per cent). Highet's estimate for England and Wales in 1951 was significantly less, 22.9 per cent, with Protestants on 16.4 per cent (against 43.4 per cent in Scotland) and Catholics on 6.4 per cent (compared with 14.5 per cent in Scotland).[20] For England alone R.D. Macleod calculated an even lower figure of 15.5 per cent in 1948 (9.8 per cent Protestant and 5.8 per cent Catholic), but this was as a proportion of the whole population.[21] Church membership figures for Wales in 1953, collated by Ivor

DOI: 10.1057/9781137512536.0007

TABLE 2.5 *John Highet's estimates of adult church membership, Scotland, 1947–66*

	1947	1951	1957	1959	1964	1966
Numbers						
Church of Scotland	1,256,167	1,271,200	1,315,600	1,315,466	1,259,162	1,233,800
Other Presbyterian	40,064	37,900	34,400	53,674	50,338	50,000
Other Protestant	190,777	202,100	203,600	170,710	170,700	172,000
Roman Catholic	472,600	505,200	525,200	530,550	539,800	545,200
All	1,959,608	2,016,400	2,078,800	2,070,400	2,020,000	2,001,000
% of adult population						
Church of Scotland	36.0	36.5	37.7	37.6	36.4	36.1
Other Presbyterian	1.2	1.1	1.0	1.5	1.5	1.5
Other Protestant	5.5	5.8	5.8	4.9	4.9	5.0
Roman Catholic	13.6	14.5	15.0	15.0	15.6	15.9
All	56.2	57.8	59.5	59.0	58.5	58.5

Note: The other Protestant total for 1947 is likely to be a slight underestimate, omitting figures for several smaller denominations.

Sources: J. Highet, *The Churches in Scotland To-Day: A Survey of Their Principles, Strength, Work, and Statements* (Glasgow: Jackson, 1950), pp. 73–6; idem, 'Scottish Religious Adherence', *British Journal of Sociology*, 4 (1953), pp. 142–59; idem, 'The Churches', in A.K. Cairncross, ed., *The Scottish Economy: A Statistical Account of Scottish Life* (Cambridge: Cambridge University Press, 1954). pp. 297–315; idem, 'The Protestant Churches in Scotland: A Review of Membership, Evangelistic Activities, and Other Aspects', *Archives de Sociologie des Religions*, 4 (1959), pp. 97–104; idem, *The Scottish Churches: A Review of Their State 400 Years after the Reformation* (London: Skeffington, 1960), pp. 54–9, 213–14; idem, 'Churchgoing in Scotland', *New Society*, 26 December 1963; idem, 'Faithful after a Fashion', *Glasgow Herald*, 11 October 1965; idem, 'How Religious Is Scotland?', *Glasgow Herald*, 5 January 1968; idem, 'Great Britain: Scotland', in H. Mol, ed., *Western Religion: A Country by Country Sociological Inquiry* (The Hague: Mouton, 1972), p. 255.

DOI: 10.1057/9781137512536.0007

Cassam, worked out at 32.2 per cent of population.[22] Successive editions of the *World Christian Handbook* during the period collected membership data from individual denominations, but not comprehensively nor with much attempt at aggregation.[23] Standard reference works of the time tended to concentrate on membership just for the largest churches.[24]

Three retrospective efforts to compute church membership for the long 1950s deserve mention. The first was by Robert Currie, Alan Gilbert, and Lee Horsley who tabulated actual and estimated membership for the principal denominations (Episcopalian, Scottish Presbyterian, major Nonconformist, and Catholic) in Britain for each year between 1945 and 1963. Total membership dipped from 8,153,000 in 1945 to 8,100,000 in 1947 before rising steadily to 9,735,000 in 1962, then dropping back to 9,669,000 in 1963. Between 1945 and 1963, therefore, membership rose by 19 per cent, which was double the rate of population growth, ostensibly confirming Brown's 'religious boom'. However, much of the increase was due to the Catholics, who grew by 48 per cent, whereas the major Protestants managed only 1 per cent overall (13 per cent for Episcopalians and 1 per cent for Scottish Presbyterians, with major Nonconformists shrinking by 13 per cent). During these years Protestant membership peaked at 5,407,000 in 1956, 6 per cent above the 1945 level; Episcopalian and Scottish Presbyterian membership likewise peaked in 1956, while the major Nonconformists contracted continuously from 1945.[25]

The second membership series was compiled by Peter Brierley, relates to the United Kingdom rather than Britain, seeks to cover all denominations (however small), and is for five-yearly intervals only. He shows total church membership falling from 9,682,000 in 1945 (26 per cent of the adult population) to 9,614,000 in 1950 (25 per cent) before rising to 9,773,000 in 1955 (25 per cent) and to 9,918,000 in 1960 (24 per cent), then dropping to 9,648,000 in 1965 (23 per cent). In other words, the member/adult population ratio was fairly stable, with little sign of religious revival, partly because Brierley used estimated Mass attendance for Catholics, rather than estimated population.[26]

The third metric, which is still evolving, is a measure of church adherence (embracing both church and Sunday school membership) devised by Brown and also employing notional Mass attendance for Catholics. The raw data have not been published, but from commentaries which are in print, per capita adherence in Scotland (for which the information seems more robust than for England and Wales) exceeded 50 per cent during the early 1950s, peaking in 1956, by which point it was only

DOI: 10.1057/9781137512536.0007

2 per cent less than in 1914 and 5 per cent less than the all-time high of 1905. The Church of Scotland performed especially well.[27]

Membership – Anglican

The picture which emerges from these overarching views of church membership, therefore, is not wholly consistent, suggesting the need for a more granular approach, commencing with the Anglicans. The Church of England's principal membership measure was the electoral roll, first introduced in 1924. Numbers on the post-war roll were much lower than in the inter-war period, both absolutely and relative to the adult population. In the latter case, the proportion of adults on the roll had peaked at 15.2 per cent as early as 1927, and it fell continuously from 9.8 per cent in 1947 (2,989,700) to 8.5 per cent in 1962 (2,793,200).[28] These rolls were revised quinquennially and thus were probably less 'dynamic' than the traditional yardstick of Anglican belonging, Easter communicants, originating in the canons of 1604. Total Easter week communicants in England stood at 1,878,000 in 1947 (equivalent to 5.8 per cent of adults aged 15 and over), climbed to 2,348,000 in 1956 (7.2 per cent), and then flattened out, being 2,347,000 in 1962 (6.9 per cent).[29] Christmas communicants – a new measure – were somewhat lower, the best year being 1960 (2,074,000 or 6.2 per cent).[30]

However, as Gill has argued, marked diachronic and synchronic fluctuations in the relationship between general church attendance and communicants considerably undermine confidence in use of the latter as a longitudinal indicator of Anglican conformity.[31] This variation was symptomatic of the differential importance attached to the sacrament across time and space. Moreover, Easter communicant numbers then, as now, were liable to be affected by purely secular circumstances such as how early or late in the year Easter Sunday fell, and by the state of the weather on the day. Unfortunately, Easter Day communicants were the only membership measure employed by the disestablished Church in Wales, rising from 155,900 in 1945 to 182,900 in 1960.[32] In Scotland, by contrast, Episcopal Church of Scotland communicants were consistently around 56,000 each year between 1945 and 1963, albeit the larger permanent membership (which included baptised children and non-communicant adult worshippers) contracted from a post-war peak of 110,800 in 1949, falling below 100,000 after 1960.[33]

DOI: 10.1057/9781137512536.0007

Data also exist for confirmands, which serve as a proxy for 'new members' in the Anglican communion. In the Church of England the number confirmed in any one year represented a very small proportion of the estimated population aged 12–20, the best figure in the post-war era being 3.4 per cent in 1954–60.[34] Expressed as a proportion of existing electoral roll members, a crude index of the annual recruitment rate, the ratio of confirmands progressively improved from 4.8 per cent in 1950 to 6.7 per cent in 1960, after which it fell back.[35] Related to the potential pool of confirmands, generally assumed to be the total of infant baptisms 13 years before, the best year for confirmands was 1953, when 42 per cent of the baptismal pool of 1940 were confirmed; otherwise, the ratio was stable at 36 or 37 per cent.[36] The majority of confirmands were women, 59 per cent between 1948 and 1963, which was two points more than in the inter-war period but hardly conclusive proof of Brown's claims about the increasing and 'extraordinarily important' role of women in driving church growth in 1948–60 which appears to be solely evidenced by Anglican confirmations.[37] Nevertheless, the cumulative impact of confirmation remained quite impressive, with almost ten million people, not far short of one-quarter of the English population, being confirmed members of the Church of England between 1956 and 1964.[38]

Membership – Catholic

Membership of the Roman Catholic Church was coterminous with the total 'baptised' Catholic population (including children), whether practising or not. This was assessed, and probably often guessed, by parish priests, so the reliability of the measure, collated at diocesan level and subsequently aggregated and preserved for posterity in the separate editions of the *Catholic Directory* for England and Wales and Scotland, should not be exaggerated. It probably excludes very nominal and lapsed Catholics who were not known to priests. Certainly, there was a surplus after the Second World War of those self-identifying as Catholics in sample surveys against the Church's population returns.[39] There were also many contemporary Catholic critics of the latter as being seriously underestimated. For example, in the late 1940s a respected academic denounced the Catholic population statistics for England and Wales in the *Catholic Directory* for their 'blatant absurdities' and as 'palpably incorrect and misleading'.[40] The situation was unchanged in the early 1960s: 'the experience of missioners and

DOI: 10.1057/9781137512536.0007

parish-priests who have conducted "Crusades for Souls", which includes a close door-to-door census, is that the Catholics known to the clergy are less than three-quarters of all the Catholics in the country ... '[41] The Scottish data were evidently no more reliable.[42]

One of the severest critics of the figures of Catholic population published in the *Catholic Directory* was Tony Spencer, who ran the NDS from 1953 until 1964 when it was wound up after the Catholic Bishops' Conference in England and Wales withdrew its support and passed some of the NDS's responsibilities to the Catholic Education Council (CEC). During his time at the NDS, and later as Director of the Pastoral Research Centre, Spencer worked tirelessly to improve the accuracy of Catholic statistics, devising several different approaches for estimating the Catholic population of Great Britain in general and England and Wales in particular, as summarized in Table 2.6. The range of estimates

TABLE 2.6   *Estimates of Roman Catholic population, Great Britain, 1948–63*

Population measure	1948	1951	1958	1963
England and Wales				
Reported – Currie *et al.*	2,528,000	2,809,000	3,343,000	3,727,000
Reported – NDS/CEC	2,649,000	2,838,000	3,422,000	4,017,000
Extrapolated from baptisms – method 1	3,687,000	3,821,000	4,260,000	4,763,000
Extrapolated from baptisms – method 2	4,436,000	4,730,000	5,569,000	6,212,000
Extrapolated from sample surveys	4,353,000	NA	NA	4,983,000
Sacramental index	NA	NA	5,270,000	5,490,000
Scotland				
Reported – Currie *et al.*	707,000	748,000	787,000	812,000
Reported – NDS/CEC	718,000	751,000	781,000	812,000
Extrapolated from sample surveys	887,000	NA	NA	986,000
Great Britain				
Reported – Currie *et al.*	3,235,000	3,557,000	4,130,000	4,539,000
Reported – NDS/CEC	3,367,000	3,589,000	4,203,000	4,829,000
Extrapolated from sample surveys	5,240,000	5,405,000	5,798,000	5,969,000

Notes: The principal difference between the two extrapolations from baptisms is that the second method corrected for net migration and took account of conversions. The sacramental index represented baptised Catholics who participated in the other rites of passage and had not dropped out of the Church.

Sources: R. Currie, A.D. Gilbert, and L. Horsley, *Churches and Churchgoers: Patterns of Church Growth in the British Isles since 1700* (Oxford: Clarendon Press, 1977), p. 153; A.E.C.W. Spencer, 'Demography of Catholicism', *The Month*, 2nd New Series, 8 (1975), p. 105; idem, 'Catholics in Britain and Ireland: Regional Contrasts', in D.A. Coleman, ed., *Demography of Immigrants and Minority Groups in the United Kingdom* (London: Academic Press, 1982), pp. 221, 227–9, 234, 238–9; idem, ed., *Digest of Statistics of the Catholic Community of England & Wales, 1958–2005: Volume 1: Population and Vital Statistics, Pastoral Services, Evangelisation, and Education* (Taunton: Russell-Spencer, 2007), pp. 18–19.

DOI: 10.1057/9781137512536.0007

is extremely wide, confirming the incompleteness of *Catholic Directory* data, although all reveal strong and consistent growth in the Catholic population during the long 1950s.

Perhaps the most meaningful measure of Catholic membership would be the sacramental index or 'four-wheeler' Catholics who participated in all the Church's rites of passage. This was not computed in Scotland until 1967,[43] but, if we assume that the same ratio between reported and sacramental index population applied in 1963 as in 1967, then the Scottish index in 1963 would have been 883,000. Added to the 5,490,000 for England and Wales, there were thus 6,373,000 sacramental Catholics in Britain in 1963 or 12.2 per cent of the whole British population (against just 8.7 per cent suggested by the *Catholic Directory* figures), with 11.7 per cent in England and 17.0 per cent in Scotland. The difference between the sacramental index and the second method of calculating the Catholic population from baptisms is explained by 'leakage', baptised Catholics who failed to participate in the sacraments. Leakage had always been difficult for the Catholic Church, but Spencer argued that it only emerged as a large-scale phenomenon in the early 1960s. Whereas only 4.5 per cent of the baptised population had been affected by it in 1958, 11.7 per cent were in 1963. According to Spencer, alienation first become prominent in 1961 and began to impact nuptiality in 1962 and fertility in 1964.[44]

Even on the imperfect *Catholic Directory* statistics, the growth in the Catholic population between 1945 and 1963 was impressive, 48 per cent in Britain, 56 per cent in England and Wales, and 22 per cent in Scotland. Spencer is helpful in illuminating the reasons for this growth, which he sees as fourfold.[45] First, mixed marriages were becoming more common, with 34 per cent of Catholics marrying in Catholic churches in 1963 taking a non-Catholic partner, up from 30 per cent over five years. Such non-Catholics may or may not have converted to Catholicism in due course, but they would have been under a commitment to raise their children in the faith.

Second, there was some evidence that the fertility of Catholics remained higher than that of non-Catholics, albeit the gap was closing.[46] Catholic avoidance of artificial means of contraception doubtless contributed to the differential, one study in 1946–47 finding that Catholic women married during the previous ten years were 18 per cent more likely than all females in the cohort not to be using birth control, 59 against 41 per cent, the 41 per cent who had taken it up being fairly evenly divided

DOI: 10.1057/9781137512536.0007

between appliance and non-appliance methods.[47] Another survey in 1954 discovered that only 47 per cent of Catholic married couples were taking birth control precautions, compared with 69 per cent of Anglicans and 79 per cent of Nonconformists.[48] As a consequence, Catholicism recorded a healthy rate of natural growth (cradle baptisms less deaths in any given year), 81,000 in England and Wales during 1959 and 97,000 in 1963.[49]

Third, there was significant migration from Catholic countries, mainly to England and Wales. The migrants came from Poland, Lithuania, Ukraine, Latvia, Yugoslavia, and Italy in the immediate aftermath of the Second World War, and most notably from Ireland between 1950 and 1960. Net emigration from the Republic of Ireland amounted to 525,000 from 1946 to 1961, the overwhelming majority of the emigrants settling in Britain, with the proportion of Irish-born in Britain increasing by 39 per cent between the censuses of 1951 and 1961. The Catholic Church's arrangements for despatching and receiving these Irish migrants were thoroughly investigated by the NDS in a critical report in 1960 which proved so controversial that it was suppressed by the Catholic authorities.[50]

Fourth, there was a modest number of conversions to Catholicism, peaking at 16,000 in England and Wales in 1959.[51] The Catholic Enquiry Service had been created in 1954 to facilitate such conversions, but, of the 100,000 who had taken its course by 1961, merely 7,300 had actually been received into the Church.[52] Most converts were probably from the Church of England, but there was also significant traffic in the other direction.[53]

Membership – Free Church and Presbyterian

Membership of the Free Churches and Presbyterian Churches was conceptually less problematic than for the Church of England and Roman Catholic Church since they mostly operated some form of 'membership' associated with the transition from adolescence to adulthood, although the age of eligibility for and criteria of membership varied. Table 2.7 collates actual figures and estimates of members for each denomination at the start and end of the long 1950s. In absolute terms, overall Free Church and Presbyterian membership reduced by 3.4 per cent over these 18 years, from (in round figures) 3,549,000 to 3,430,000. Relative to the estimated adult population aged 15 and over, the fall was from 9.6 per cent in 1945 to

DOI: 10.1057/9781137512536.0007

TABLE 2.7   *Actual and estimated membership of Free Churches and Presbyterian Churches, Great Britain, 1945 and 1963*

Denomination	c. 1945	c. 1963	% change	Source
Baptists				
Baptist Union – England	222,000	187,402	−15.6	Author/C&C
Baptist Union – Wales	113,000	87,660	−22.4	Author/C&C
Baptist Union – Scotland	21,500	18,952	−11.9	Author/C&C
Strict and Particular Baptists	10,000	8,000	−20.0	Author/FCD
Old Baptist Union	1,000	750	−25.0	UKCH/UKCH
Sub-total	*367,500*	*302,764*	*−17.6*	
Congregationalists				
Congregational Union – England	230,163	187,239	−18.6	C&C/C&C
Congregational Union – Wales	155,382	120,663	−22.3	C&C/C&C
Congregational Union – Scotland	37,283	32,194	−13.6	C&C/C&C
Sub-total	*422,828*	*340,096*	*−19.6*	
Methodists				
Methodist Church – England	690,088	657,787	−4.7	C&C/C&C
Methodist Church – Wales	48,735	39,676	−18.6	C&C/C&C
Methodist Church – Scotland	13,836	13,311	−3.8	C&C/C&C
Independent Methodists	9,043	8,111	−10.3	WA/WA
Wesleyan Reform Union	6,122	5,571	−9.0	WCH/WA
Sub-total	*767,824*	*724,456*	*−5.6*	
Presbyterians				
Presbyterian Church of England	67,563	69,852	+3.4	C&C/C&C
Presbyterian Church of Wales	172,954	127,814	−26.1	C&C/C&C
Church of Scotland	1,259,927	1,268,887	+0.7	C&C/C&C
United Free Church of Scotland	23,863	21,779	−8.7	C&C/C&C
Free Church of Scotland	5,500	5,750	+4.5	Author/Author
Free Presbyterian Church of Scotland	680	600	−11.8	Highet/WCH
United Original Secession Church of Scotland	1,953	NA	NA	C&C/NA
Reformed Presbyterian Church of Scotland	704	548	−22.2	WCH/C&C
Sub-total	*1,533,144*	*1,495,230*	*−2.5*	
Pentecostalists				
Apostolic Church	5,200	5,000	−3.8	WCH/WCH
Assemblies of God	18,250	21,000	+15.1	WCH/FCD
Elim Church	14,700	20,000	+36.1	Highet/WCH
New Testament Church of God	NA	2,000	NA	NA/Author
Other Pentecostal groups	2,000	4,000	+100.0	Author/Author
Sub-total	*40,150*	*52,000*	*+29.5*	
Other Free Churches				
Christian Brethren	80,000	98,000	+22.5	WA/UKCH
Churches of Christ	12,101	7,257	−40.0	C&C/C&C
Church of the Nazarene	1,000	3,501	+250.1	Author/C&C
Countess of Huntingdon's Connexion	1,200	1,000	−16.7	WCH/FCD

Continued

DOI: 10.1057/9781137512536.0007

TABLE 2.7   *Continued*

Denomination	c. 1945	c. 1963	% change	Source
Fellowship of Independent Evangelical Churches	9,000	16,000	+77.8	UKCH/UKCH
Free Church of England	5,000	4,155	−16.9	Author/FCFC
Lutherans	10,000	14,000	+40.0	Author/UKCH
Moravian Church	3,502	3,186	−9.0	C&C/C&C
Salvation Army	123,000	102,000	−17.1	Highet/UKCH
Sub-total	*244,803*	*249,099*	*+1.8*	
Other Nonconforming Churches				
Catholic Apostolic Church	500	100	−80.0	Author/Author
Christadelphians	18,000	20,000	+11.1	UKCH/UKCH
Christian Scientists	10,000	11,000	+10.0	Author/Author
Jehovah's Witnesses	11,622	47,053	+304.9	C&C/C&C
Latter-day Saints	5,933	55,719	+839.1	C&C/C&C
New Church	5,035	3,815	−24.2	C&C/C&C
Quakers	20,534	21,126	+2.9	C&C/C&C
Seventh Day Adventists	6,372	10,084	+58.3	C&C/C&C
Spiritualists	46,000	50,000	+8.7	Highet/Author
Unitarians	24,000	17,000	−29.2	WCH/UKCH
Other smaller denominations	25,000	30,000	+20.0	Author/Author
Sub-total	*172,996*	*265,897*	*+53.7*	
TOTAL	*3,549,245*	*3,429,542*	*−3.4*	

Notes: The United Original Secession Church of Scotland mostly joined the Church of Scotland in 1956. The New Testament Church of God commenced in 1953. Independent Methodist members include junior members.

Sources: Author = estimate by author; C&C = R. Currie, A.D. Gilbert, and L. Horsley, *Churches and Churchgoers: Patterns of Church Growth in the British Isles since 1700* (Oxford: Clarendon Press, 1977), appendix; CYB = *Christian Year Book*, 1947; FCD = *Free Church Directory*, 1965–66; FCFC = *Free Church Federal Council Annual Report and Directory*, 1964; Highet = John Highet, *The Churches in Scotland To-Day: A Survey of Their Principles, Strength, Work, and Statements* (Glasgow: Jackson, 1950), p. 74, 'Scottish Religious Adherence', *British Journal of Sociology*, 4 (1953), p. 148, *The Scottish Churches: A Review of Their State 400 Years after the Reformation* (London: Skeffington, 1960), pp. 213–14; UKCH = P.W. Brierley, ed., *UK Christian Handbook, Religious Trends, No. 2, 2000/01 Millennium Edition* (London: Christian Research, 1999); WA = *Whitaker's Almanack*, 1946, 1964; WCH = *World Christian Handbook*, 1949, 1962.

8.6 per cent in 1963. The historic Free Churches suffered most, and nowhere more so than in Wales, where the Calvinistic Methodists contracted by 26.1 per cent, Baptists by 22.4 per cent, Congregationalists by 22.3 per cent, and (Wesleyan) Methodists by 18.6 per cent.[54] In Britain the Congregational decline was relentless, year on year, with the number of Congregational members in England falling below the Baptist total for the first time in 1952

DOI: 10.1057/9781137512536.0007

and consistently from 1955.[55] It would have been a similarly depressing story for the Baptists and Methodists in Britain, were it not for extremely modest and temporary recoveries in 1954–56 and 1948–54, respectively. Moreover, membership in these bodies was predominantly female, as it had been in earlier periods and would be in immediately ensuing years[56]; for instance, a sample of 16 Congregational church lists for 1946–59 indicated 65 per cent of members were women.[57] Additionally, local surveys demonstrated that a significant minority of Free Church members was non-worshipping and, consequently, to be reckoned as 'dead wood'.[58] Tellingly, asked outright whether they thought membership returns were genuine, only 29 per cent of Methodist ministers in the Manchester and Stockport District in 1962 gave an unqualified affirmative answer.[59]

Of the major denominations, the Church of Scotland fared best of all, for, although its growth was minimal (0.7 per cent) taking the period as a whole, communicants rose by 5 per cent from 1947 to 1956 and active communicants by 9 per cent from 1948 to 1955. Nevertheless, a sizeable minority of the Kirk's members failed to take Communion at least annually, typically almost one-third and as many as 42 per cent in 1945 (doubtless reflecting wartime conditions), so commitment was often quite nominal. Pentecostalists expanded by 29.5 per cent, under-pinned by immigration from the West Indies, which was at its height between 1951 and 1962; the more mainstream denominations – Anglican, Catholic, or Free Church – to which West Indians had been attached in the Caribbean held out little appeal once they had settled in England.[60] Pentecostal growth was probably curtailed by the difficulties which West Indians had in adjusting to the English climate, which led them to stay indoors as much as possible in the winter.[61] Most successful, absolutely, were some (but not all) of the smaller and/or newer independent or sectarian bodies, with Jehovah's Witnesses (from 1948) and Latter-Day Saints (from 1957) enjoying spectacular progress.

The foregoing are all net figures ('stocks'), the balance of year-on-year gains and losses ('flows'). Flows are of fundamental importance but have not featured much in the debate about religious change during the long 1950s, although they have been studied in two denominations.[62] Some sense of the underlying dynamics of non-Anglican Protestant member-ship can be gauged from Table 2.8, charting cumulative annual inflows and outflows between 1945 and 1963 in the four denominations (three Presbyterian) which collected this information. This demonstrates that an ostensibly modest aggregate decline of 85,000 in net membership

DOI: 10.1057/9781137512536.0007

over 18 years in reality concealed huge movements, comprising gains of 2,649,000 and losses of 2,734,000. There is no reason to believe such large-scale turnover was untypical of Free Churches as a whole. In this way, far more adults than might be imagined were touched by Free Church and Presbyterian membership. Very many will have been members for a relatively short period; lifelong membership was probably not the norm.

In terms of specific flows, the recruitment of new members was superficially healthy, even in the Methodist Church and Presbyterian Church of Wales (which were declining). They averaged 75,000 per annum for the four denominations combined, consistently exceeding deaths. The mean annual recruitment rate (new members as a proportion of all members the previous year) for the entire period was 3.5 per cent for the Methodist Church, 3.4 per cent for the Church of Scotland (including restorations), 3.0 per cent for the Presbyterian Church of England, and 2.3 per cent for the Presbyterian Church of Wales and for the Baptists (for whom there are returns of adult baptisms[63]). Recruitment rates tended to be highest during the first part of our period, dropping from the mid-1950s, the Baptists and Church of Scotland seemingly experiencing peaks associated with Billy Graham's crusades at that time. For

TABLE 2.8   *Aggregate membership turnover in four non-Anglican Protestant Churches, Great Britain, 1945–63*

	Methodist Church	Presbyterian Church of England	Presbyterian Church of Wales	Church of Scotland	All four Churches
Gains					
New/restored members	493,889	39,416	66,587	837,495	1,437,387
Transfers	310,059	79,700	71,084	750,967	1,211,810
Total	*803,948*	*119,116*	*137,671*	*1,588,462*	*2,649,197*
Losses					
Deaths	245,633	21,965	53,215	392,596	713,409
Transfers	364,034	40,471	74,464	773,425	1,252,394
Others	238,393	56,678	56,395	416,441	767,907
Total	*848,060*	*119,114*	*184,074*	*1,582,462*	*2,733,710*
Net Change					
Transfers	−53,975	+39,229	−3,380	−22,458	−40,584
Other changes	+9,863	−39,227	−43,023	+28,458	−43,929
Total	*−44,112*	*+2*	*−46,403*	*+6.000*	*−84,513*

Source: R. Currie, A.D. Gilbert, and L. Horsley, *Churches and Churchgoers: Patterns of Church Growth in the British Isles since 1700* (Oxford: Clarendon Press, 1977), pp. 170, 176, 179–80, 187.

DOI: 10.1057/9781137512536.0007

the most part, new members appear to have been recruited from the children of existing members, a reducing source in the face of smaller families arising from deferred marriage and the increasing practice of family limitation.[64]

Net transfer losses (the difference between in- and out-transfers) particularly affected the Methodist Church, which lost track of around 3,000 members each year when they relocated from one area to another. The Church of Scotland lost just over 1,000 annually in this way, but many of them were probably migrating to England where they often joined the Presbyterian Church of England, which gained a net 2,000 members each year through transfer. Deaths in these four denominations accounted for 26 per cent of crude losses or 47 per cent after adjusting for in-transfers. They had the greatest impact in the Methodist Church and Presbyterian Church of Wales, whose mean mortality rates for these years were 17.5 and 18.3 per 1,000, respectively (against 16.1 for the Church of Scotland and 16.6 for the Presbyterian Church of England). Detailed investigation of the Methodist data has demonstrated that the proportion of losses attributable to death had been steadily rising since the 1910s and the mortality rate from the 1920s. This was not because Methodists had a lower life expectancy than anybody else (the contrary may have been the case)[65] but because their congregations were ageing, thus moving into cohorts which were more likely to die, making their population pyramid progressively top-heavy.[66] The other main category of losses was, in Methodist parlance, the 'ceased to meet', those who had resigned their membership or had their name removed from the roll for non-participation. The Presbyterian Church of England suffered especially badly through such losses, averaging 4.3 per cent a year, the other three denominations recording rates between 1.7 and 1.9 per cent, although the lower rate may have reflected a reluctance by church authorities to remove people. In Methodism, according to surveys in the Manchester and Stockport and Sheffield Districts in 1962, more than four-fifths of the 'ceased to meet' had not been in effective contact with the Church for over two years and over one-half were under 40 years of age.[67]

Such membership flows connect to another characteristic Free Church phenomenon, that of adherents. All denominations had formerly attracted substantial numbers of people who maintained close links with a chapel, often as regular worshippers and financial supporters, while stopping short of a commitment to formal membership, but

DOI: 10.1057/9781137512536.0007

they became a dying breed in the twentieth century.[68] In England and Wales, the only hard evidence about adherents from the long 1950s is for the Presbyterian Church of Wales, those in the 'whole congregation' who were not members reducing from 62,500 (27 per cent) in 1945 to 36,700 (22 per cent) in 1963. Deducting 'children of the church' and probationer members, it has been estimated that non-member adult attendants represented just 8 per cent of the whole congregation in 1945 and 4 per cent in 1963.[69] The Methodist Church's constituency in Britain was assessed at 2,500,000 in 1954[70] and 2,100,000 in 1962,[71] but these figures seem hard to square with its community roll which, when first introduced in 1969, enumerated only 1,165,000 individuals, including 635,000 members.[72] Moreover, the roll included children and others in pastoral care who were not adherents in the traditional sense. The same limitation applies to the *World Christian Handbook* which estimated the worshipping community as approximately double membership for the Baptists and Congregationalists and treble for the Methodists.[73] Certainly, William Pickering, in undertaking his research in two industrial towns, reckoned that less than one-tenth of adults at Free Church services in the 1950s were non-members.[74] In Scotland, by contrast, adherents had always been less numerous, since the tradition had mainly been confined to the Free Church of Scotland and Free Presbyterian Church of Scotland and some Church of Scotland parishes in the North and North West of Scotland. Notwithstanding, Highet reckoned that there could be up to 500,000 adult adherents in Scotland in all Churches (alongside roughly two million full members), which seems a rather excessive figure and difficult to reconcile with the specific denominational examples cited by Highet.[75] Perhaps one might more plausibly suggest 1,000,000 Free Church and Presbyterian adult adherents by *c.* 1963, two-thirds the total *c.* 1939.[76]

Membership – Sunday schools

Besides adherents, children associated with the Free Churches and Presbyterian Churches (and with the Episcopalian Churches) also need to be factored into any picture of religious belonging, especially as reflected in Sunday school membership. The Protestant Sunday school movement had been in recession for a long time and had failed to keep pace with population increase since the 1880s. It had lost considerable

DOI: 10.1057/9781137512536.0007

ground between the wars[77] and been further disrupted by the evacuation of children during the Second World War. The post-war 'baby boom' (most marked in 1946–48) held out the prospect of resurgence, and there was, indeed, some absolute growth in Free Church Sunday schools for a few years (with the conspicuous exception of the Presbyterian Church of Wales). The Free Church Federal Council reported an increase of 5 per cent in its scholars between 1948 and 1953, albeit it was insufficient to prevent a fall in the proportion of the population aged 3–17 attending its schools (from 16.5 to 15.5 per cent).[78] Peaks for individual denominations included 1952 for Methodists, 1953 for Baptists, and 1954 for Congregationalists and the Presbyterian Church of England.[79] In the Church of Scotland Sunday school growth was sustained until 1956 and was especially large (32 per cent since 1945), with Bible class membership also on the up (if somewhat erratically), the post-war peak for both series momentarily returning to pre-war levels.[80]

Rapid decline then ensued, and by 1963 the combined Sunday scholars of the five principal English and Welsh Free Churches were, at 949,000, 33 per cent less than they had been in 1945 and 39 per cent less than in 1953. Average attendance at Sunday schools did not necessarily fall in parallel (in the Methodist case, it actually rose, from 69 per cent of enrolment in 1945 to 73 per cent in 1963),[81] but comparatively few scholars (one in ten in the Free Churches) stayed on until their fourteenth birthday and a mere one in seven progressed to church membership.[82] Statistics of Church of England Sunday scholars are available only for four years – 1953, 1956, 1958, and 1960 – and fell by 21 per cent over these seven years, from 17.7 to 13.3 per cent of persons aged 3–14.[83] These and other data gaps mean that a definitive picture of Sunday school membership is beyond our grasp. It should be noted that the annual statistics of schools and scholars affiliated to the National Sunday School Union by no means tell the full story, even for England and Wales.[84] However, Brierley offers us estimates for the United Kingdom, total scholars for all denominations expanding from 3,583,000 in 1945 to 3,635,000 in 1950 before steadily reducing to 2,336,000 in 1965; relative to the population under 15 years, he calculates the fall from 33 per cent in 1945 to 19 per cent in 1965.[85] The contraction in the late 1950s and early 1960s, which occurred notwithstanding another increase in crude birth rates, has been attributed to changing family activities on Sunday in general and to greater car ownership in particular.[86]

DOI: 10.1057/9781137512536.0007

As with church membership, we are dealing with net figures, which give no indication of the flows of Sunday school membership. For that we need to turn to the claims made in sample surveys. Nationally representative polls by M-O in July 1948[87] and Gallup in December 1954[88] and February 1957[89] suggested that 90–94 per cent of adults had gone to Sunday school as a child, albeit 11 per cent (1954) had only been for a short time and 17 per cent (1957) had not attended regularly. The likelihood of childhood Sunday school attendance was slightly greater for women than men, older than younger generations, and among current churchgoers than non-churchgoers. Whereas 19 per cent of non-churchgoers in 1954 had only been to Sunday school for a short time, this was the case with just 3 per cent of frequent churchgoers. For those aged 16–29, 11 per cent of 1954 interviewees had never been to Sunday school and 12 per cent in 1957, with an additional 27 per cent of the same age cohort at the latter date having merely gone sometimes. Contemporary investigations also suggested that, among secondary school pupils, Sunday school was disproportionately appealing to girls than boys, younger than older pupils, and the educationally more able than less able.[90]

The overwhelming majority of Britons (86 per cent according to M-O in 1948, 95 and 92 per cent according to Gallup in 1954 and 1957, respectively) approved of children going to Sunday school. The main reasons given (in 1948) were for religious and moral teaching (53 per cent), because it was a 'good thing' (22 per cent), and as somewhere to go on Sundays (19 per cent). However, there was increasing sensitivity to children's wishes, with 57 per cent in 1957 qualifying their approval of Sunday schools with the caveat 'providing they want to', although a minority (35 per cent) insisted children should go even if they did not want to. Certainly, not all Sunday school attendance was voluntary, 33 per cent of a Wellingborough sample recalling that they had been compelled to go to Sunday school and a further 28 per cent being put under some pressure to do so.[91] Reported Sunday school attendance by respondents' own children exceeded one-half in national surveys in September 1947 (Research Section of Odhams Press),[92] December 1954 (Gallup), February 1957 (Gallup), summer 1961 (Independent Television Authority),[93] and December 1963–January 1964 (Gallup).[94] This was likewise true of more specialist samples: readers of *The People* in 1951,[95] residents of Greater Derby in 1953,[96] and married women with children in 1954.[97] It is probable

DOI: 10.1057/9781137512536.0007

that, as with other reports of socially respectable behaviour, these claims may have been inflated.

Membership – other religions

This completes the analysis of religious membership in the Anglican, Catholic, Free, and Presbyterian Churches, but other religious communities also require brief consideration. Membership of the various Orthodox traditions grew, through immigration, after the Second World War, from an estimated 51,000 in 1945 to 133,000 in 1965.[98] Jews were the principal non-Christians, the most credible figures for them being around 450,000 (including 50,000 wartime refugees) at the commencement of the long 1950s and 410,000 at the end, two-thirds of them at the latter date in the London region. Although numbers were reducing, especially in the provinces, this apparently had little to do with emigration to Israel following its establishment in 1948 (only 5,397 UK Jews had emigrated there by the end of 1963)[99] and more with a falling Jewish birth rate and ageing Jewish population.[100] The growth of the Muslim community was almost entirely linked with immigration. Just after the Second World War there were no more than 30,000 Muslims in Britain, and probably less, but post-war labour shortages, the partition of India and other overseas developments which created refugee problems, and the settlement rights conferred on Commonwealth citizens by the British Nationality Act 1948 fuelled immigration from South Asia from the late 1950s. By 1961 there were an estimated 50,000 Muslims in England and Wales according to Ceri Peach and Richard Gale, disproportionately men, but with a big influx of dependents immediately thereafter, in a bid to beat tighter controls introduced by the Commonwealth Immigrants Act 1962.[101] Sikhs started from an even lower base, no more than 1,000 or 2,000 in Britain in 1945, but numbers rose through immigration to 7,000 in 1951 and 16,000 in 1961.[102] Peach and Gale's estimate for Hindus in 1961 was 30,000, but most came later as a result of Africanization policies in Kenya, Tanzania, and Uganda between 1965 and 1972. A long tail of other non-Christian religions probably did not amount to more than 5,000 individuals in 1960.[103]

Finally, we need to note membership of non-faith bodies. Three were longstanding: National Secular Society (dating back to 1866), Ethical Union (1896), and Rationalist Press Association (RPA, 1899). All had relatively

DOI: 10.1057/9781137512536.0007

small paid-up memberships by the long 1950s. The RPA's membership first peaked at 5,010 in 1947, fell to 2,878 in 1956, and then recovered to 4,726 in 1963. It was predominantly male, middle class, and often short-lived, over half of the members surveyed in 1961 having joined the RPA during the previous five years. The Ethical Union had just 417 members in 1959 and 918 in 1963. The National Secular Society, with a commitment to militant atheism and historically a working-class following, has always been sensitive about publishing the number of its members, but they cannot have exceeded 5,000 at this time. A more overtly humanist strand emerged during the 1950s, starting with the formation of local humanist groups in 1954–55 (under the auspices of the Ethical Union), which had adopted the name humanist by 1956–57. This new movement culminated in the foundation of the British Humanist Association (BHA) in May 1963 as a common front for the Ethical Union and RPA (which had also shifted from rationalism to humanism, although it withdrew from the BHA in 1966). The BHA recruited 824 members by the end of 1963, 1,706 by April 1964, and 2,898 by April 1965. Given that the memberships of these bodies partially overlapped, there were probably no more than 10,000 individuals in total who belonged to organized irreligion in the early 1960s.[104] Public awareness of 'any organization which represents the views of humanists, agnostics, and atheists' was also very low, 1 per cent, according to National Opinion Polls in April–May 1964.[105]

Notes

1   C.D. Field, 'Measuring Religious Affiliation in Great Britain: The 2011 Census in Historical and Methodological Context', *Religion*, 44 (2014), pp. 357–82; A.J. Christopher, 'The Religious Question in the United Kingdom Census, 1801–2011', *Journal of Ecclesiastical History*, 65 (2014), pp. 601–19.

2   *Church Times*, 23 November 1945.

3   *Hansard, Commons*, 4 May 1960, cols. 1193–6. Relevant papers are in The National Archives, RG 19/223.

4   A.E.C.W. Spencer, 'Numbering the People: Should the Census Ask about Religion?', *The Tablet*, 22 April 1961.

5   J. Gould and S. Esh, eds, *Jewish Life in Modern Britain* (London: Routledge and Kegan Paul, 1964), p. 135.

6   M. Stacey, *Tradition and Change: A Study of Banbury* (London: Oxford University Press, 1960), pp. 57–73; S. Bruce, 'A Sociology Classic Revisited: Religion in Banbury', *Sociological Review*, 59 (2011), pp. 201–22.

DOI: 10.1057/9781137512536.0007

7   A common formulation was 'what is your religious denomination?'
This rather implied that respondents both had a religion and could
denominationalize it, which probably helped to drive down the number who
professed no religion.

8   In an England only survey (Gallup, December 1963–January 1964) the
Anglican proportion was two-thirds; Social Surveys (Gallup Poll), *Television
and Religion* (London: University of London Press, 1964), pp. 10, 131.

9   Field, 'Measuring Religious Affiliation', pp. 371–2.

10   However, they accounted for only 4 per cent of all young adults aged 15–24 in
urban England (Young Christian Workers, January–February 1957); A.E.C.W.
Spencer, 'Youth and Religion', *New Life*, 14 (1958), p. 24.

11   Gallup, *GIPOP*, i., p. 404.

12   W.S.F. Pickering, 'The Place of Religion in the Social Structure of Two
English Industrial Towns (Rawmarsh, Yorkshire and Scunthorpe,
Lincolnshire)' (PhD thesis, University of London, 1958), chapter VI; idem,
'Quelques résultats d'interviews religieuses', in Conférence Internationale de
Sociologie Religieuse, *Vocation de la sociologie religieuse: sociologie des vocations*
(Tournai: Casterman, 1958), pp. 54–76; idem, ' "Religious Movements" of
Church Members in Two Working-Class Towns in England', *Archives de
Sociologie des Religions*, 11 (1961), pp. 129–40.

13   T.M. Owen, 'Chapel and Community in Glan-llyn, Merioneth', in E. Davies
and A.D. Rees, eds, *Welsh Rural Communities* (Cardiff: University of Wales
Press, 1960), p. 228.

14   For example, E. Lewis-Faning, *Report on an Enquiry into Family Limitation and
Its Influence on Human Fertility during the Past Fifty Years* (Papers of the Royal
Commission on Population, 1, London: HMSO, 1949), p. 46.

15   The following data have all been calculated from the British Social Attitudes
Information System at http://www.britsocat.com/. There has also been
separate analysis by birth cohort of religious affiliation *at the time of interview*
recorded in BSA surveys for 1983–2008; see S. McAndrew, 'Religious
Affiliation by Birth Decade', *British Religion in Numbers*, 25 March 2011, http://
www.brin.ac.uk/news/2011/religious-affiliation-by-birth-decade/, with associated
data tables at http://www.brin.ac.uk/figures/#AffiliationAttendance. However, by
definition, this cannot take account of changes in affiliation between the period
of growing up and interview.

16   M.E.J. Wadsworth and S.R. Freeman, 'Generation Differences in Beliefs: A
Cohort Study of Stability and Change in Religious Beliefs', *British Journal of
Sociology*, 34 (1983), pp. 421–2.

17   Calculated from the British Election Studies Information System at http://
www.besis.org/.

18   Calculated from the Centre for Comparative European Survey Data
Information System at http://www.ccesd.ac.uk/Home.

DOI: 10.1057/9781137512536.0007

19 The 1947 figure is almost certainly too low, with actual or estimated data seemingly lacking for some smaller denominations.

20 J. Highet, 'Scottish Religious Adherence', *British Journal of Sociology*, 4 (1953), p. 144; idem, 'The Churches', in A.K. Cairncross, ed., *The Scottish Economy: A Statistical Account of Scottish Life* (Cambridge: Cambridge University Press, 1954), p. 299.

21 R.D. Macleod, 'Church Statistics for England', *Hibbert Journal*, 46 (1948), pp. 351–7.

22 I. Cassam, 'An Analysis of Church Affiliations in Wales', *Western Mail and South Wales News*, 30 January 1953.

23 *World Christian Handbook*, 1949, p. 243; 1952, pp. 129–30; 1957, pp. 13–14; 1962, pp. 208–10.

24 For example, A.M. Carr-Saunders, D.C. Jones, and C.A. Moser, *A Survey of Social Conditions in England and Wales as Illustrated by Statistics* (Oxford: Clarendon Press, 1958), pp. 263–4; A. Sampson, *Anatomy of Britain* (London: Hodder and Stoughton, 1962), pp. 160–73; D.E. Butler and J. Freeman, *British Political Facts, 1900–1960* (London: Macmillan, 1963), pp. 200–4 and *British Political Facts, 1900–1968* (3rd edition, London: Macmillan, 1969), pp. 296–301; *The Reader's Digest Complete Atlas of the British Isles* (London: Reader's Digest Association, 1965), pp. 120–1.

25 R. Currie, A.D. Gilbert, and L. Horsley, *Churches and Churchgoers: Patterns of Church Growth in the British Isles since 1700* (Oxford: Clarendon Press, 1977), p. 32.

26 P.W. Brierley, ed., *UK Christian Handbook, Religious Trends, No. 2, 2000/01 Millennium Edition* (London: Christian Research, 1999), p. 8.17. Other versions of this table (with slight variations) appear in P.W. Brierley, *A Century of British Christianity: Historical Statistics, 1900–1985* (Bromley: MARC Europe, 1989), p. 26; idem, *Religion in Britain, 1900 to 2000* (London: Christian Research, 1998), p. 3; idem, 'Religion', in A.H. Halsey and J. Webb, eds, *Twentieth-Century British Social Trends* (Basingstoke: Macmillan, 2000), pp. 654–5.

27 C.G. Brown, 'Religion and Secularisation', in T. Dickson and J.H. Treble, eds, *People and Society in Scotland, III, 1914–1990* (Edinburgh: John Donald, 1992), pp. 48–54, 79; idem, 'A Revisionist Approach to Religious Change', in S. Bruce, ed., *Religion and Modernization: Sociologists and Historians Debate the Secularization Thesis* (Oxford: Clarendon Press, 1992), pp. 42–6; idem, *Religion and Society in Scotland since 1707* (Edinburgh: Edinburgh University Press, 1997), pp. 61–6, 158–9; idem, *Religion and the Demographic Revolution: Women and Secularisation in Canada, Ireland, UK, and USA since the 1960s* (Woodbridge: Boydell Press, 2012), pp. 90–3.

28 R.F. Neuss, *Facts and Figures about the Church of England, Number 3* (London: Church Information Office, 1965), p. 59; Currie et al., *Churches*, p. 129.

DOI: 10.1057/9781137512536.0007

29   Neuss, *Facts*, p. 60; W.S.F. Pickering, 'The Present Position of the Anglican and Methodist Churches in the Light of Available Statistics', in W.S.F. Pickering, ed., *Anglican-Methodist Relations: Some Institutional Factors* (London: Darton, Longman & Todd, 1961), pp. 8–10.

30   *Statistical Supplement to the Church of England Yearbook*, 1978, p. 16.

31   R. Gill, *The 'Empty' Church Revisited* (Aldershot: Ashgate, 2003), pp. 13, 124.

32   J. Williams, *Digest of Welsh Historical Statistics* (2 vols, Cardiff: Welsh Office, 1985), ii, pp. 257–8; D.D. Morgan, *The Span of the Cross: Christian Religion and Society in Wales, 1914–2000* (Cardiff: University of Wales Press, 1999), p. 189.

33   Currie et al., *Churches*, p. 129.

34   Neuss, *Facts*, p. 55; Currie et al., *Churches*, pp. 167–8; D.A. Martin, 'Interpreting the Figures', in M. Perry, ed., *Crisis for Confirmation* (London: SCM Press, 1967), pp. 106–15.

35   Currie et al., *Churches*, pp. 129, 167–8. The index is crude in that the minimum age for electoral roll membership was 18 until 1956 (17 thereafter), whereas the mean age of confirmands was typically a little younger (albeit nearly one-fifth in 1958 and 1960 were 21 and over – Neuss, *Facts*, p. 55).

36   Currie et al., *Churches*, pp. 167–8; Pickering, 'Present Position', pp. 12–13.

37   C.G. Brown, 'Masculinity and Secularisation in Twentieth-Century Britain', in Y.M. Werner, ed., *Christian Masculinity: Men and Religion in Northern Europe in the 19th and 20th Centuries* (Leuven: Leuven University Press, 2011), p. 49. There was no appreciable gender imbalance among confirmands in the Roman Catholic Church, nor any sign that it was increasing, the proportion of female confirmands being 51 per cent in both 1958 and 1963; A.E.C.W. Spencer, ed., *Digest of Statistics of the Catholic Community of England & Wales, 1958-2005, Volume 1: Population and Vital Statistics, Pastoral Services, Evangelisation, and Education* (Taunton: Russell-Spencer, 2007), p. 93.

38   D.H. Doig, *The Membership of the Church of England: Changes in Recent Years* (London: Church Information Office, 1960), p. 3; Neuss, *Facts*, p. 58; *Statistical Supplement to the Church of England Yearbook*, 1978, p. 16.

39   Table 2.1; A.E.C.W. Spencer, 'Catholics in Britain and Ireland: Regional Contrasts', in D.A. Coleman, ed., *Demography of Immigrants and Minority Groups in the United Kingdom* (London: Academic Press, 1982), p. 228.

40   W.A. Zbyszewski, letter in *Catholic Herald*, 3 May 1946; idem, 'The Catholics of England and Wales: The Reasons for Thinking They May Be Ten Per Cent of the Population', *The Tablet*, 6 March 1948.

41   Anon, 'How Many Catholics in England and Wales?' *Catholic Truth*, 6 (1962), p. 5; *Catholic Herald*, 8 June 1962.

42   F. Macmillan, 'The Faithful of Scotland: A Statistical Enquiry', *The Tablet*, 25 July 1959.

DOI: 10.1057/9781137512536.0007

43 A.E.C.W. Spencer, *Report on the Parish Register, Religious Practice & Population Statistics of the Catholic Church in Scotland, 1967* (Harrow: Pastoral Research Centre, 1969), pp. 5–7.

44 A.E.C.W. Spencer, 'Demography of Catholicism', *The Month*, 2nd New Series, 8 (1975), pp. 102–5; idem, 'Alienation in English Catholicism, 1958–1972', in A.E.C.W. Spencer and P.A. O'Dwyer, eds, *Proceedings of the Second Annual Conference, Sociological Association of Ireland, Dublin, 4–5 April 1975* (Belfast: Department of Social Studies, Queen's University of Belfast, 1976), pp. 115–34. Cf. W.N.T. Roberts, 'Why Do Catholics Lapse? I. The Size of the Problem', *The Tablet*, 9 May 1964.

45 A.E.C.W. Spencer, 'The Demography and Sociography of the Roman Catholic Community of England and Wales', in L. Bright and S. Clements, eds, *The Committed Church* (London: Darton, Longman & Todd, 1966), pp. 73–7; idem, 'Demography of Catholicism', pp. 100–5.

46 Social Surveys (Gallup Poll), *Television and Religion*, pp. 13–14, 81–2; R.-C. Chou and S. Brown, 'A Comparison of the Size of Families of Roman Catholics and Non-Catholics in Great Britain', *Population Studies*, 22 (1968), pp. 51–60.

47 Lewis-Faning, *Report on an Enquiry*, pp. 81–2.

48 E. Chesser, *The Sexual, Marital, and Family Relationships of the English Woman* (London: Hutchinson's Medical Publications, 1956), p. 269.

49 Spencer, ed., *Digest of Statistics*, p. 74. For Scotland, see J. Darragh, 'The Catholic Population of Scotland, 1878–1977', in D. McRoberts, ed., *Modern Scottish Catholicism, 1878–1978* (Glasgow: Burns, 1979), p. 241.

50 A.E.C.W. Spencer (M.E. Daly, ed.), *Arrangements for the Integration of Irish Immigrants in England and Wales* (Dublin: Irish Manuscripts Commission, 2012); idem, *Services for Catholic Migrants, 1939–2008: Background Data from the Archives and Databank of the Newman Demographic Survey and the Pastoral Research Centre* (Taunton: Russell-Spencer, 2008). More generally, see J.A. Jackson, *The Irish in Britain* (London: Routledge & Kegan Paul, 1963), pp. 135–51; and E. Delaney, *The Irish in Post-War Britain* (Oxford: Oxford University Press, 2007), pp. 129–69.

51 Currie et al., *Churches*, pp. 190–1.

52 Sampson, *Anatomy*, p. 171.

53 Doig, *Membership*, p. 3; Neuss, *Facts*, p. 54.

54 Morgan, *Span of the Cross*, pp. 205–19 on the crisis of Welsh Nonconformity, 1945–62.

55 For background, see D.M. Thompson, *The Decline of Congregationalism in the Twentieth Century* (London: Congregational Memorial Hall Trust, 2002).

56 C.D. Field, 'Adam and Eve: Gender in the English Free Church Constituency', *Journal of Ecclesiastical History*, 44 (1993), pp. 63–79; idem, 'Zion's People:

DOI: 10.1057/9781137512536.0007

Who Were the English Nonconformists? Part 1: Gender, Age, Marital Status, and Ethnicity', *Local Historian*, 40 (2010), pp. 91–112.

57   Calculated from printed and manuscript lists for churches in Ashton-under-Lyne, Birmingham, Bolton, Bradford, Brightlingsea, Brighton, Lindfield, London, Manchester, Northampton, and Torquay. For local examples of the gender balance in the membership of other denominations, see Pickering, 'Place of Religion', p. XIV.30. The Quakers were perhaps the least gendered of the Free Churches, but even they averaged a membership which was 57 per cent female between 1945 and 1965; Yearly Meeting of the Religious Society of Friends (Quakers) in Britain, *Tabular Statement as at 31 xii 2012*, p. 11, http://www.quaker.org.uk/files/Tabular-statement-2013-web.pdf.

58   For example, *Methodist Church Conference Agenda*, 1962, p. 267; Morgan, *Span of the Cross*, p. 211; I.M. Randall, *The English Baptists of the Twentieth Century* (Didcot: Baptist Historical Society, 2005), p. 280.

59   'Lapsed Members in the Manchester District' (1962), unpublished report in author's possession.

60   C. Hill, *West Indian Migrants and the London Churches* (London: Oxford University Press, 1963); S.C. Patterson, *Dark Strangers: A Sociological Study of the Absorption of a Recent West Indian Migrant Group in Brixton, South London* (London: Tavistock Publications, 1963), pp. 252–62, 349–62, 438–9; R.B. Davison, *Black British: Immigrants to England* (London: Oxford University Press, 1966), pp. 128–9; C.R. Taylor, 'British Churches and Jamaican Migration: A Study of Religion and Identities, 1948 to 1965' (PhD thesis, Anglia Polytechnic University, 2002); C.R. Potter [née Taylor], 'Is Home Where the Heart Is? Jamaican Migration and British Churches, 1948–1965', *Wesley Historical Society of London and the South East Journal*, 80 (2011), pp. 4–13.

61   M.J.C. Calley, *God's People: West Indian Pentecostal Sects in England* (London: Oxford University Press, 1965), pp. 43–4.

62   J.N. Wolfe and M. Pickford, *The Church of Scotland: An Economic Survey* (London: Geoffrey Chapman, 1980), pp. 80–6; C.D. Field, 'Joining and Leaving British Methodism since the 1960s', in L.J. Francis and Y. Katz, eds, *Joining and Leaving Religion: Research Perspectives* (Leominster: Gracewing, 2000), pp. 57–85.

63   Currie et al., *Churches*, pp. 164–5, 190–1 (Britain); Brierley, *UK Christian Handbook, Religious Trends, No. 2*, p. 9.4 (England and Wales).

64   For a Methodist case study, see C.D. Field, 'Demography and the Decline of British Methodism: I. Nuptiality', *Proceedings of the Wesley Historical Society*, 58 (2012), pp. 175–89; idem, 'Demography and the Decline of British Methodism: II. Fertility', *Proceedings of the Wesley Historical Society*, 58 (2012), pp. 200–15.

DOI: 10.1057/9781137512536.0007

65 C.D. Field, 'Long-Living Methodists', *British Religion in Numbers*, 24 June 2010, http://www.brin.ac.uk/news/2010/long-living-methodists/.

66 C.D. Field, 'Demography and the Decline of British Methodism, III: Mortality', *Proceedings of the Wesley Historical Society*, 58 (2012), pp. 247–63.

67 Field, 'Joining', pp. 59–60, 68; 'Lapsed Members in the Manchester District'; J.R. Butler, 'A Sociological Study of Lapsed Membership', *London Quarterly and Holborn Review*, 191 (1966), pp. 236–44; B.E. Jones, *Family Count: A Study Pamphlet About Methodism Today* (London: Methodist Church Home Mission Department, 1970), pp. 8–9.

68 P.J. Yalden, 'Association, Community, and the Origins of Secularisation: English and Welsh Nonconformity, *c.* 1850–1930', *Journal of Ecclesiastical History*, 55 (2004), pp. 296–300.

69 Currie et al., *Churches*, pp. 77, 151, 179–80.

70 I.L. Holt and E.T. Clark, *The World Methodist Movement* (Nashville: The Upper Room, 1956), p. 137.

71 *Minutes of the Annual Conference of the Methodist Church*, 1962, p. 104.

72 *The Methodist Church Triennial Statistical Report, 1969–71* (London: the Church, 1972), pp. 2–3.

73 *World Christian Handbook*, 1952, pp. 129–30; 1957, pp. 13–14; 1962, pp. 208–10.

74 Pickering, 'Place of Religion', pp. IV.34–5.

75 J. Highet, *The Churches in Scotland To-Day: A Survey of Their Principles, Strength, Work, and Statements* (Glasgow: Jackson, 1950), pp. 7, 19, 25; idem, 'Scottish Religious Adherence', p. 143; idem, 'The Churches', p. 298; idem, *The Scottish Churches: A Review of Their State 400 Years after the Reformation* (London: Skeffington, 1960), pp. 25, 27, 209–12; Wolfe and Pickford, *Church of Scotland*, p. 70.

76 C.D. Field, 'Gradualist or Revolutionary Secularization? A Case Study of Religious Belonging in Inter-War Britain, 1918–1939', *Church History and Religious Culture*, 93 (2013), p. 91.

77 Ibid., pp. 85–7.

78 *Sunday Schools Today: An Investigation of Some Aspects of Christian Education in English Free Churches* (London: Free Church Federal Council, [1956]), p. 34.

79 Currie et al., *Churches*, pp. 176, 179–80, 187, 190–1.

80 Ibid., p. 170; J. Sutherland, *Godly Upbringing: A Survey of Sunday Schools and Bible Classes in the Church of Scotland* (Edinburgh: Church of Scotland Youth Committee, 1960).

81 *Minutes of the Annual Conference of the Methodist Church*, 1946, p. 195; 1964, p. 114. The main example of a local pan-denominational census of Sunday school attendance in the 1950s is for Rawmarsh and Scunthorpe; Pickering, 'Place of Religion', Appendix 7.

82 *Sunday Schools Today*, pp. 6–7.

83 Currie et al., *Churches*, pp. 167–8; Neuss, *Facts*, p. 61.

DOI: 10.1057/9781137512536.0007

84   N. Stanton, 'From Sunday Schools to Christian Youth Work: Young People's Engagement with Organised Christianity in Twentieth Century England and the Present Day' (PhD thesis, Open University, 2013), pp. 85–96.

85   Brierley, *Century of British Christianity*, p. 48; idem, *UK Christian Handbook, Religious Trends, No. 2*, p. 2.15; idem, ed., *UK Church Statistics, 2005–2015* (Tonbridge: ADBC Publications, 2011), p. 14.4.8.

86   D. Rosman, 'Sunday Schools and Social Change in the Twentieth Century', in S. Orchard and J.H.Y. Briggs, eds, *The Sunday School Movement: Studies in the Growth and Decline of Sunday Schools* (Milton Keynes: Paternoster, 2007), p. 159.

87   *Daily Graphic*, 10 August 1948; M-OA, 1/2/47/12C.

88   BBC Audience Research Department, 'Religious Broadcasts and the Public: A Social Survey of the Differences between Non-Listeners and Listeners to Religious Broadcasts' (1955), pp. 24–7, BBC Written Archives Centre, Caversham.

89   *News Chronicle*, 15 April 1957; Gallup, *GIPOP*, i., pp. 404, 407.

90   For example, University of Sheffield Institute of Education, *Religious Education in Secondary Schools: A Survey and a Syllabus* (London: Thomas Nelson, 1961), p. 85; K.E. Hyde, *Religious Learning in Adolescence* (Edinburgh: Oliver and Boyd, 1965), pp. 7–8.

91   D. Wright, *Attitudes towards the Church in Wellingborough* (Leicester: Department of Adult Education, Leicester University, 1965), p. 24.

92   *News Review*, 6 November 1947.

93   Independent Television Authority, *Religious Programmes on Independent Television* (London: the Authority, 1962), p. 55.

94   Social Surveys (Gallup Poll), *Television and Religion*, pp. 89–91, 129–30.

95   G.E.S. Gorer, *Exploring English Character* (London: Cresset Press, 1955), pp. 246–7, 454–5.

96   T. Cauter and J. Downham, *The Communication of Ideas: A Study of Contemporary Influences on Urban Life* (London: Chatto & Windus, 1954), pp. 54–5.

97   Chesser, *Sexual, Marital, and Family Relationships*, p. 286.

98   Brierley, *UK Christian Handbook, Religious Trends, No. 2*, pp. 2.8, 8.11, 8.18.

99   According to statistics collected by the Jewish Agency for Israel and available at http://jafi.org/JewishAgency/English/About/Press+Room/Aliyah+Statistics/jul27.htm.

100   H. Neustatter, 'Demographic and Other Statistical Aspects of Anglo-Jewry', in M. Freedman, ed., *A Minority in Britain: Social Studies of the Anglo-Jewish Community* (London: Vallentine, Mitchell, 1955), pp. 59, 73–6, 132; S.J. Prais and M. Schmool, 'The Size and Structure of the Anglo-Jewish Population, 1960-65', *Jewish Journal of Sociology*, 10 (1968), pp. 5–34; *Jewish Year Book*, 1945, p. 307; 1947, pp. 297–300; 1964, pp. 191, 193–5.

DOI: 10.1057/9781137512536.0007

101 C. Peach and R. Gale, 'Muslims, Hindus, and Sikhs in the New Religious Landscape of England', *Geographical Review*, 93 (2003), p. 479; H. Ansari, '*The Infidel Within*': *Muslims in Britain since 1800* (London: Hurst, 2004), pp. 50–1; S. Gilliat-Ray, *Muslims in Britain: An Introduction* (Cambridge: Cambridge University Press, 2010), pp. 44–52.

102 G. Singh and D.S. Tatla, *Sikhs in Britain: The Making of a Community* (London: Zed Books, 2006), pp. 49–52, 59.

103 Brierley, *UK Christian Handbook, Religious Trends, No. 2*, pp. 10.6–10.8.

104 C.B. Campbell, 'Membership Composition of the British Humanist Association', *Sociological Review*, 13 (1965), pp. 327–37; idem, 'Humanism in Britain: The Formation of a Secular Value-Oriented Movement', in D.A. Martin, ed., *A Sociological Yearbook of Religion in Britain, 2* (London: SCM Press, 1969), pp. 157–72; idem, *Toward a Sociology of Irreligion* (London: Macmillan, 1971), pp. 83, 88, 92–3; S. Budd, 'The Humanist Societies: The Consequences of a Diffuse Belief System', in B.R. Wilson, ed., *Patterns of Sectarianism: Organisation and Ideology in Social and Religious Movements* (London: Heinemann, 1967), pp. 366–405; idem, *Varieties of Unbelief: Atheists and Agnostics in English Society, 1850–1960* (London: Heinemann, 1977), p. 181; Currie et al., *Churches*, pp. 194–5.

105 'National Opinion Polls National Political Surveys', dataset at UKDA [distributor], SN 64009.

DOI: 10.1057/9781137512536.0007

3
Behaving

Abstract: *Various measures of religious behaviour are examined. The evidence for church attendance, the traditional yardstick of religious practice, is reviewed from three separate perspectives: church data, local surveys, and opinion polls. Demographic and other variations affecting churchgoing are noted. The reach of public worship was extended by audiences for religious broadcasts on the radio and television, and by participation in the rites of passage (baptisms, churchings, marriages, and funerals), the statistics of which are analysed. Finally, opinion polls provide limited insights into private religious practices, especially Bible ownership and reading and prayer.*

Keywords: Bible; church attendance; religious behaviour; religious broadcasting; religious practice; rites of passage

Field, Clive D. *Britain's Last Religious Revival? Quantifying Belonging, Behaving, and Believing in the Long 1950s.* Basingstoke: Palgrave Macmillan, 2015. DOI: 10.1057/9781137512536.0008.

DOI: 10.1057/9781137512536.0008

Church attendance – introduction

The traditional yardstick of religious behaving was church attendance. In theory, it posed fewer consistency problems than church membership since it was a universal measure, recognized by all Christian denominations at that time as a valid and necessary public expression of religious commitment (even if not all 'ordinary' Christians viewed it in that light). A pervasive contemporary view, epitomized by the Archbishop of York, was that churchgoing had declined over a long period and continued to do so, with the problem spreading to suburbs and villages and the upper class, all of which had previously been fairly immune. The trend was attributed in part to the disruptive effects of two world wars but mostly to social changes and alternative leisure pursuits.[1] At the same time, the aggregate numbers claimed for churchgoing remained impressive. Thus, R.C. Churchill estimated 7,000,000 regular or frequent churchgoers in 1954, together with a further 5,000,000 occasional ones,[2] while there were still thought to be 11,800,000 regular worshippers at the end of the period.[3] Such figures implied a measure of stability in church attendance during the long 1950s, which is the conclusion of a sociologist of religion retrospectively reviewing the fragmentary evidence in 1972[4] and, more recently, seemingly of Brown.[5] Unfortunately, there were no systematic investigations on which such commentators could draw for a definitive assessment. The ostensible exception, M-O's report on *Contemporary Churchgoing* for the *British Weekly* in 1948–49, was in reality a rather limited and primarily qualitative exercise, costing no more than £120 and focusing on 'the faithful fifth' who attended regularly. It repurposed existing M-O material, supplemented by religious life histories of its panel members, observations of individual churches (especially in London), and a postal questionnaire to an unrepresentative sample of Protestant clergy and laity (which elicited a very poor response).[6] A fresh evaluation of all relevant data on church attendance is thus long overdue, whether collected by the churches, through local surveys, or national opinion polls.

Church attendance – church data

There had been no England-wide census of churchgoing since 1851, and the next would not occur until 1979, when one was undertaken

DOI: 10.1057/9781137512536.0008

by the Nationwide Initiative in Evangelism. Neither did the Church of England commence a record of its all-age Usual Sunday Attendance until 1968, when it stood at 1,606,000 or 3.5 per cent of the population.[7] This renders somewhat improbable Leslie Paul's suggestion of an Average Sunday Attendance of 3,000,000 in 1962, derived from a 10 per cent sample survey of Anglican parishes.[8] Back-projecting from 1968, 2,000,000 would seem altogether more plausible. It was later still (1972) before the Methodist Church inaugurated its return of average attendance in October, there being 510,200 attendances at all services that year (12 per cent less than the membership), of which 339,900 were at the principal service (41 per cent below membership).[9] This echoed a study of Methodism's rural circuits 14 years earlier, which revealed that average congregations were around two-thirds of membership.[10] If these member/attender ratios held good for the early 1960s, and if they were also characteristic of Free Churches as a whole, as William Hodgkins contended in 1960,[11] then overall Free Church attendances in England each week would have been of the order of 1,500,000.

In the Roman Catholic Church 11 of 18 dioceses in England and Wales appear to have been recording Mass attendance by 1956. Scaling up for the other seven, on the basis of the ratio of Massgoers to Catholic population for the 11 dioceses, Mass attendance on a typical Sunday can be calculated at around 1,650,000 in 1956, much the same as the estimated number making their Easter confession (1,680,000).[12] This was equivalent to 50 per cent of the entire Catholic population (as published in the *Catholic Directory*), somewhat higher than the 35–36 per cent of baptised Catholics aged seven and over suggested by the NDS for 1957.[13] Certainly, Mass attendance was growing strongly in these years. In the Archdiocese of Southwark it rose by 56 per cent in the late 1940s, to reach 66 per cent of the Catholic population by 1949,[14] while the Dioceses of Cardiff, Leeds, Liverpool, Menevia, and Southwark returned an aggregate increase of 10 per cent between 1957 and 1960.[15]

As part of its rationalization of Catholic statistics in England and Wales, the NDS first incorporated Mass attendance in its parochial form in 1959 (asking for figures for 10 January 1960), but participation was slow, and not until 1963 did all dioceses collect data. Allowing for gaps, there was a total Mass attendance of just over 2,000,000 on an ordinary Sunday in the early 1960s, which, discounting for young children, Tony Spencer equated to 41 per cent of the Catholic population aged 7 and over.[16] This proportion accorded both with the guestimate of *Catholic*

Truth and with censuses conducted in 13 English parishes in the early 1960s.[17] It was higher (53 per cent or 435,000) in Scotland in 1967, according to Spencer,[18] the only year after 1959 (see later) for which Scottish Mass attendance is available, Motherwell being the sole diocese to collect it on a routine basis.

Summarizing the church-based statistics for *c.* 1960, the following picture emerges. In England average attendances on a typical Sunday were 2,000,000 in the Church of England, 1,500,000 in the Free Churches, and 2,000,000 in the Catholic Church, 5,500,000 in all or 13 per cent of the whole population. In Wales the Council for Wales and Monmouthshire obtained estimates from the principal denominations (Anglican, Catholic, and four Free Church) in 1961 of the number of communicants and 'regular worshippers' (defined as frequenting twelve services a year), the resultant total of 576,000 (167,000 Anglican, 340,000 Free Church, 69,000 Catholic) being equivalent to 22 per cent of the Welsh population.[19] In Scotland, and similarly based on returns from the various church authorities, Highet calculated that adults attending at least one service on Sunday in 1959 amounted to 911,000 (472,000 Presbyterian, 105,000 other Protestant, 334,000 Catholic) or 26 per cent of the adult population.[20] For Britain there were thus more than 7,000,000 church attenders each week or 14 per cent of the population (allowing for child churchgoers in Scotland and the lesser Free Churches in Wales).

Church attendance – local surveys

As a cross-check on these estimates, but also as an illustration of local diversity, it is essential to review the limited number of censuses of churchgoing in particular places. Table 3.1 summarizes those for urban Britain, all the English locations being industrial towns and districts with the exceptions of York and some of the Liverpool wards. All the censuses set out to record attendances on an ordinary Sunday, but there were differences between them as regards methodology and completeness, affecting comparability. As a rough generalization, it might be said that weekly churchgoing in urban England was of the order of 10–15 per cent, with higher figures attributable to a strong Catholic presence (e.g., 82 per cent of worshippers in the Liverpool wards were Catholics, 60 per cent in Billingham, and 44 per cent in the Birmingham suburb). Glasgow apart, the censuses enumerated morning and evening services, so there will have been some double-counting of attenders ('twicing'), which had far from died out at this time (M-O reporting in 1949 that 26 per cent of Anglicans and 75 per cent in the Free Churches still attended more than one service on Sunday).[21] In Scunthorpe and Rawmarsh adjustments for twicing reduced attendance/population ratios to, respectively, 7.5–8.5 per cent and 6–7.5 per cent.[22]

Proper trend data are only available for York, where the proportion of adults in church on a typical Sunday was 4.7 points lower in 1948 than 1935 (17.7 per cent); for the Church of England alone attendances recorded in visitation returns fell from 8.6 per cent of the total

TABLE 3.1   *Church attendance, urban Great Britain, 1947–64*

Year	Place	Total population	Covered population	Attendances as % of covered population
1947	High Wycombe	40,600	Adults	10.5
1948	York	78,500	Adults	13.0
1948–49	Coseley	32,000	Adults	14.0
1953–54	Glossop	18,000	All	11.9
1954	Glasgow	1,083,000	Adults	20.1
1954	Scunthorpe	56,520	All	10.1
1955	Rawmarsh	19,450	All	8.4
1959	Billingham-on-Tees	28,000	Adults	15.6
1963–64	Birmingham (suburb)	20,500	All	17.7
1964	Liverpool (four wards)	79,300	All	17.3

Sources: BILLINGHAM-ON-TEES: P.R. Kaim-Caudle, *Religion in Billingham, 1957–59* (Billingham-on-Tees: Billingham Community Association, 1962), pp. 5–9; BIRMINGHAM: K.A. Busia, *Urban Churches in Britain: A Question of Relevance* (London: Lutterworth Press, 1966), pp. 27, 111, 153; COSELEY: D. Rich, 'Spare Time in the Black Country', in L. Kuper, ed., *Living in Towns* (London: Cresset Press, 1953), p. 330; GLASGOW: J. Highet, 'The Churches in Glasgow', *British Weekly*, 22 August 1957; idem, 'The Churches', in J. Cunnison and J.B.S. Gilfillan, eds, *The Third Statistical Account of Scotland: Glasgow* (Glasgow: Collins, 1958), pp. 728–34, 956–7; and idem, *The Scottish Churches: A Review of Their State 400 Years after the Reformation* (London: Skeffington, 1960), pp. 62–3, 103–4; GLOSSOP: A.H. Birch, *Small-Town Politics: A Study of Political Life in Glossop* (London: Oxford University Press, 1959), p. 177; HIGH WYCOMBE: B.S. Rowntree and G.R. Lavers, *English Life and Leisure: A Social Study* (London: Longmans, Green, 1951), pp. 345, 403–4, 413–14 and York, University of York, Borthwick Institute for Archives, LTE 30/1, 45/1-3; LIVERPOOL: W. Shannon, 'A Geography of Organised Religion in Liverpool' (BA dissertation, University of Liverpool, 1965), p. 49; RAWMARSH: W.S.F. Pickering, 'The Place of Religion in the Social Structure of Two English Industrial Towns (Rawmarsh, Yorkshire and Scunthorpe, Lincolnshire)' (PhD thesis, University of London, 1958), tables 5–9, 31; SCUNTHORPE: as Rawmarsh; YORK: Rowntree and Lavers, *English Life*, pp. 341–5 and York, University of York, Borthwick Institute for Archives, LTE 44/1-5 (and LTE 42/1-5, 43/1 for an abandoned 1947 census).

DOI: 10.1057/9781137512536.0008

population in 1931 to 4.2 per cent in 1947, then rose to 4.8 per cent in 1953 before declining again.[23] There was a similar Anglican pattern in Hull, with a fall from 3.9 per cent in 1931 followed by an increase from 1.7 to 1.8 per cent between 1947 and 1953, with figures of 2.4 per cent of the population in Sheffield in 1956 and 2.1 per cent in 1961.[24] A less systematic comparison for Bolton in 1937 and 1960 pointed to a general decline among Protestants, but perhaps more so for membership than attendance.[25]

In three towns (Billingham, Rawmarsh, and Scunthorpe) congregations were counted on Easter Day as well as on an ordinary Sunday, the former figures being 44 per cent above the latter overall, but with significant denominational variation (117 per cent for Anglicans, 25 per cent for Free Churches, and 11 per cent for Catholics). A gender breakdown of adult worshippers is available for eight places (Billingham, Birmingham, High Wycombe, Rawmarsh, Scunthorpe, York, as well as the Redfield district of Bristol and Rotherham),[26] revealing an imbalance of women: 58 per cent in total, 54 per cent for Catholics, 57 per cent for Anglicans, and 62 per cent in the Free Churches. Overall, far from being more gendered, there were actually 2 per cent *fewer* women worshippers than in a comparable basket of inter-war censuses.[27] Disaggregation by age is provided for High Wycombe, Rawmarsh, Scunthorpe, and York,[28] revealing that 35 per cent of adult congregants were already above 50 years, peaking at 44 per cent in the Free Churches, with just 22 per cent among Catholics. A social class breakdown of male worshippers was only attempted for Rawmarsh and Scunthorpe, confirming that one-fifth came from Registrar General classes I and II (professional and managerial occupations), twice the proportion in the two towns, rising to 34 per cent for Anglicans (with 8 per cent for Catholics).

Churchgoing levels in the English countryside were thought by contemporaries to have remained somewhat higher than in towns and cities.[29] This certainly appears to have generally been the case, according to the best evidence we have for this period, Peter Varney's survey in south Norfolk in 1962. Here, despite the relative weakness of Roman Catholicism, average attendances on Sunday represented 16 per cent of the population. However, there was a wide range (from 4 to 38 per cent) in individual parishes. Congregations at festivals were as high as 33 per cent (ranging from 3 to 89 per cent).[30] Irregular attendance was felt to be a particular problem in English villages,[31] exemplified in the Hertfordshire parish of Little Munden in 1950, where 10 per cent of

DOI: 10.1057/9781137512536.0008

residents worshipped weekly, 30 per cent irregularly, and 60 per cent not at all.[32] In a South Cambridgeshire village in 1963 usual attendance was only about 9 per cent of the population.[33] Regrettably, the two classic English rural community studies of the 1950s, by Bill Williams of Gosforth, Cumbria in 1951,[34] and Northlew, Devon, in 1958,[35] do not include viable data about churchgoing *per se* (despite otherwise extensive coverage of religion), although religious practice and Sabbath observance in Gosforth were apparently lax.

In Wales three-quarters of Protestant congregations surveyed in 1951 were found to have decreased by more than half during the previous 40–50 years, occupancy of sittings averaging just 15–20 per cent.[36] A Swansea study in 1960 demonstrated that churchgoing was significantly greater among Welsh than among non-Welsh speakers,[37] and it appeared to have remained high in several Welsh-speaking villages surveyed during the 1950s, even if decline was also in evidence. In Glan-llyn, Merioneth, in 1950 up to two-thirds of the population were regular attenders.[38]

For Scotland Highet's census of Glasgow churchgoing (Table 3.1) was the single most ambitious enterprise of the long 1950s, enumerating congregations on three Sundays in each of three consecutive years (1954–56), although it was confined to the principal Sunday service (generally the morning) and to the eight major denominations (seven in 1955–56 after the Catholics withdrew support). Glasgow was a notably Catholic city, with 12.5 per cent of its adults attending Catholic churches on a typical Sunday in 1954, compared with 7.6 per cent at Protestant ones. On the back of the Billy Graham crusade, the Protestant share climbed to 9.2 per cent across the three Sundays in 1955 (and to 9.8 per cent on 1 May, the day after the crusade finished with a great rally at Hampden Park) before falling back to 8.5 per cent in 1956. Notwithstanding the strong Catholic presence, churchgoing in Glasgow, as so often the case with large cities, was probably lower than elsewhere in Scotland, and this is confirmed by Highet's 1959 national sample census (discussed earlier), with its attendance rate of 26 per cent of the adult population.

Church attendance – opinion polls

A third source of information about churchgoing, besides church data and local censuses, comprises national sample surveys of the adult population of Great Britain.[39] Setting aside purely technical considerations (such as sampling error), these need to be used with circumspection, for two main reasons. First, the claims made by respondents about their church attendance cannot be independently verified and are almost certainly subject to inflation, on account of the social respectability which still surrounded religion during this period. As M-O commented in 1947: 'There is a certain prestige value attached to *saying* one goes to church, even if one has not been for many months or hardly at all for several years... there is a tendency for those who *ever* attend church to exaggerate the frequency with which they go...'[40] Or, as Kathleen Bliss expressed it the following year: 'People want to make some kind of adjustment of what they do to what they intend to do, or think they ought to do, or think that others think they ought to do.'[41] Second, there was very little standardization in the questions which were asked about churchgoing and in the frequency categories used for analysis. So, although there is a reasonable number of surveys on the subject for the long 1950s, establishing comparability between them is problematical. Table 3.2 illustrates the apparent inconsistency and variability of results arising from such methodological challenges.

TABLE 3.2   *Claimed frequency of churchgoing in sample surveys of adults, Great Britain, 1947–63 (percentages across)*

Date	Agency	N	Weekly	Monthly	Occasionally	Never
9/1947	Odhams Press	3,019	14	8	28	50
12/1947	Gallup	2,000	20	10	30	40
7/1948	M-O	2,055	18	21	25	35
9/1948	Daily Express	?	20	8	48	24
12/1954	Gallup	1,859	25	12	24	39
3/1955	Daily Express	?	24	7	49	20
2/1957	Gallup	2,261	NA	28	22	50
3/1960	Gallup	1,000	23	19	21	37
5-8/1963	BMRB	2,009	17	10	50	23

Sources: 9/1947 = *News Review*, 30 October, 6 November 1947; 12/1947 = Gallup, *GIPOP*, i., p. 166; 7/1948 = *Daily Graphic*, 10–11 August 1948, M-OA, 1/2/47/10E, 1/2/47/12C; 9/1948 = *Daily Express*, 20 September 1948; 12/1954 = BBC Audience Research Department, 'Religious Broadcasts and the Public: A Social Survey of the Differences between Non-Listeners and Listeners to Religious Broadcasts' (1955), pp. 13–18, BBC Written Archives Centre, Caversham; 3/1955 = *Daily Express*, 19 March 1955; 2/1957 = *News Chronicle*, 16–17 April 1957, R. Stark, 'Class, Radicalism, and Religious Involvement in Great Britain', *American Sociological Review*, 29 (1964), pp. 698–706, C.Y. Glock and R. Stark, *Religion and Society in Tension* (Chicago: Rand McNally, 1965), pp. 193–9; 3/1960 = P. Alan, 'The Statistics of Belief', *The Humanist*, 76 (1961), p. 171; 5-8/1963 = 'Political Change in Britain, 1963–1970', dataset at UKDA [distributor], SN 44 – analysis by B. Clements.

DOI: 10.1057/9781137512536.0008

In fact, there are four clusters of churchgoing questions in the surveys. The simplest form was posed by M-O in April–May 1948 and December 1955–January 1956: 'What Church, if any, do you usually attend?' In reply, 75 and 81 per cent, respectively, indicated that they attended some church, rather suggesting the question was meant and/or interpreted as a loose proxy for religious affiliation (an impression reinforced by the denominational codes used for categorization), and rendering it virtually useless as a measure of religious behaving.[42] Potentially more helpful was the question genre which enquired whether respondents attended a place of worship and, if so, with what frequency. Table 3.2 reports nine exemplars for 1947–63, from which it can be seen that, very approximately, one-quarter to one-third of adults said they attended at least once a month, with wildly fluctuating proportions (anything up to one-half, depending upon the definition of the word employed in each case) 'never' attending. Weekly churchgoing on this measure was typically one-fifth to one-quarter, but the aspirational nature of this claim is inferred by a third indicator, the question posed by Gallup about activities undertaken on the Sunday prior to interview. In Britain the number stating they had attended church 'last Sunday' was 15 per cent in September–October 1948,[43] 14 per cent in February 1957,[44] and 12 per cent in May 1958[45] (with 8 per cent in England and Wales in May 1952[46] and 10 per cent in England in December 1963–January 1964).[47] Compared with the data in Table 3.2, these Sunday activity findings probably reflect something like reality. A fourth type of question concerned churchgoing history, suggesting the overall direction of travel. It confirmed that most non-churchgoers (at the time of interview) had previously attended services and that many churchgoers admitted to being less regular worshippers than they once were (Odhams Press, September 1947;[48] Gallup, December 1954,[49] February 1957,[50] December 1963–January 1964[51]).

Some of the surveys in Table 3.2 were disaggregated by demographics. Overall, females were one and a half times more likely than males to attend weekly (Odhams Press, September 1947; M-O, July 1948; *Daily Express* Poll, September 1948; Gallup, September–October 1948, December 1954). This was much the same as on the eve of the Second World War.[52] However, women's attendance fell away somewhat when they got married, set up a home, and started a family.[53] The oldest age cohorts (fifties and over) were the most frequent worshippers, followed by the very youngest (late teens and early twenties), with the middle-aged the worst (Odhams Press, September 1947; M-O, July 1948; Gallup,

December 1954). Relatively high attendance among the elderly was also suggested by several cohort studies in Birmingham in 1948[54] and c. 1956,[55] in Torquay in 1956,[56] in Aberdeen in 1958–61,[57] and nationally in 1962.[58] That the churches had not entirely lost contact with early adults was demonstrated by Research Services, 18 per cent of the 16–24s in the late 1950s recording attendance at religious services over the previous week compared with 12 per cent of over-25s.[59] Notwithstanding, two-thirds of Birmingham adolescents in the late 1940s seldom or never went to church, with girls being more likely than boys to go occasionally rather than not at all.[60] In a national sample of 15- to 19-year-olds in 1962–63, 65 per cent of young men and 55 per cent of young women never frequented public worship, with a further 17 and 24 per cent going occasionally.[61] Stereotypical social class effects on churchgoing were reaffirmed by Odhams Press in 1947, with weekly attendance of 19 per cent by the upper middle and middle classes, 16 per cent by the lower middle classes, and 13 per cent by the working classes. Similarly, ten years later, Gallup reported a range of attendance at least now and again from 39 per cent in the working class to 73 per cent in the upper class.[62]

The Odhams Press survey found a small differential for rural over urban areas, as did the *Daily Express* Poll in 1948. Post-war urban redevelopment, and the resettlement of families to new housing estates, appears to have disrupted churchgoing patterns. Certainly, interview evidence from Oxford[63] and Bristol[64] in the 1950s points to a post-removal reduction from pre-removal levels, although this effect was avoided by the Catholic Church in Liverpool which had made provision for an influx of the faithful to the Kirkby estate.[65] More granular analysis of urbanization by M-O in 1948 indicated a rather bigger margin between rural districts at one end of the spectrum and London at the other. The capital's reputation for historically low rates of churchgoing was further illustrated in other contemporary studies, including a very large-scale survey by David Glass in the Associated Rediffusion Television area in 1960.[66] Within London there were significant contrasts between middle- and working class communities.[67] In regional terms more generally, church attendance was highest in Wales and Scotland during the late 1940s (Odhams Press, September 1947; M-O, July 1948; Gallup, September–October 1948). Denominationally, Catholics were several times more likely than Anglicans to worship on a weekly basis, with the Free Churches and Church of Scotland occupying an intermediate position (Odhams Press, September 1947; M-O, July 1948; *Daily Express* Poll, September

DOI: 10.1057/9781137512536.0008

1948; Gallup, September–October 1948, December 1954). For instance, in British Market Research Bureau's survey of May-August 1963, 73 per cent of Catholics attested that they attended church at least once a month versus 45 per cent of Free Church affiliates, 39 per cent of Church of Scotland, and 16 per cent of Anglicans.[68]

Religious broadcasting

Sample surveys also shed light on another feature of the period, the way in which the reach of 'public' worship had been extended by the advent of televised religious broadcasting during the early 1950s, initially by the BBC and subsequently Independent Television.[69] Programming was varied, sometimes studio-based and sometimes in the form of outside broadcasts, and embracing services, hymn-singing, discussions, uplifting talks, and drama. The phenomenon was not new, of course, since the broadcasting of services and other religious programmes had occurred on the radio from the 1920s, and there had already been much debate in the inter-war years about whether this was partly responsible for the fall in churchgoing, through creating a competitor 'attraction' and potential 'substitute' for genuine public worship.[70] To an extent, this debate remained live after 1945. There were certainly many people – 47 per cent in Britain in September 1947 (Odhams Press)[71] and 38 per cent in England in December 1963–January 1964 (Gallup)[72] – who regarded radio and televised services respectively as a substitute for churchgoing, with still higher proportions among occasional or non-attenders. There was also a very small number in Gallup polls – 7 per cent in February 1957[73] and 4 per cent in December 1963–January 1964[74] – who acknowledged their 'churchgoing' was limited to listening to broadcast religious services only.

The BBC was sensitive to the charge that its religious services might be undermining church attendance, and Francis House (Head of Religious Broadcasting from 1947 to 1955) was at pains to demonstrate from methodologically imperfect evidence in 1948 that churchgoers were a minority of the audience for all religious broadcasts, that such broadcasts extended the evangelistic opportunities of the Churches, and that clergy did not generally consider broadcast services had a deleterious effect on churchgoing.[75] The following year the BBC (and *British Weekly*) rejected M-O's overtures for funding of a detailed investigation

DOI: 10.1057/9781137512536.0008

into the popular impact of religious broadcasting,[76] but in December 1954 the BBC did commission Gallup to undertake a representative survey of the public.[77] This revealed that, among frequent listeners to religious broadcasts, 32 per cent were frequent churchgoers, 40 per cent were occasional churchgoers, and 28 per cent were non-churchgoers; of non-listeners, 57 per cent were also non-churchgoers. In Greater Derby in February–April 1953, 56 per cent reported listening to a Sunday or weekday radio service in the seven days prior to interview, of whom less than one in eight had been to church the previous Sunday.[78]

Gallup's 1954 study for the BBC had classified 37 per cent of British adults as frequent listeners of religious broadcasts (peaking at 44 per cent of housewives and 54 per cent of over-65s), 31 per cent as occasional listeners, and 32 per cent as non-listeners (rising to 50 per cent of the 16–20 age group). By February 1957 (Gallup) non-listeners/non-viewers of religious services stood at 29 per cent (47 per cent of under-30s versus 24 per cent of over-30s), with 28 per cent tuning in regularly and 43 per cent sometimes.[79] Superficially, both sets of figures represented a contraction in the audience for religious broadcasts since September 1947 (Odhams Press), when just 16 per cent self-identified as non-listeners, with 27 per cent listening regularly and 57 per cent occasionally (albeit most of the latter confessed to doing so 'because the wireless happens to be on').[80] By December 1963–January 1964 (Gallup), non-listeners/non-viewers had risen again, to 50 per cent in England, although only 10 per cent branded broadcast religious services 'a waste of time'.[81] The Independent Television Authority's 1961 research had also uncovered 90 per cent acceptance of the desirability of televised religious programmes, yet its audience for them was confined to 'heavy viewers' who were 'glued to the ITV screen anyhow'. However, it did derive satisfaction from reaching semi- and unskilled manual workers in numbers proportionate to the population, as well as more men than were drawn to the Churches.[82]

Moving from self-reported listening and viewing, which might have been exaggerated, to official estimates of the audience size for individual religious broadcasts, we find that the aggregate audience for the five principal and longest-running BBC religious radio programmes (of which *People's Service* and *Sunday Half Hour*, both on the Light Programme, were the most popular) fell continuously from a peak of 58 per cent of adults in 1947 to 19 per cent in 1960, then stabilizing to 1963 at 17 per cent of the population aged five and over.[83] Many would

DOI: 10.1057/9781137512536.0008

have listened to more than one programme, of course, so these statistics incorporate double-counting. House estimated, from listener interviews, that just over one-third of adults in 1948 and 1952 heard at least one religious programme on Sundays, which he translated into an audience of 12–13 million, double the figure (he reckoned) who attended church, and of a much more working-class character.[84] As for television religious broadcasts, the BBC's offering began with *Meeting Point* in 1956, which initially attracted 6–7 per cent of adults. But its big success story was *Songs of Praise* (community hymn-singing),[85] launched in October 1961, whose following amounted to 11 per cent of the over-five population by 1963, only slightly below that for *People's Service* on the radio. A further 10 per cent watched *Meeting Point* and/or a Sunday morning service, bringing the BBC's total for televised religious broadcasts to 21 per cent (three points ahead of the radio). Independent Television calculated its ratings differently, as the proportion of homes able to receive its services who were tuned in for its religious programmes, the number increasing from 10 per cent in 1957 to 24 per cent in 1960 before falling back to 17 per cent in 1963. *Sunday Break* and *About Religion* were its two main draws.[86]

Notwithstanding the greater number of religious programmes available, on radio or television, by the end of the long 1950s, it seems probable that some contraction in their combined audience occurred during the decade. It also seems fairly unlikely that religious broadcasts were responsible for more than a minimal amount of the decline in churchgoing. Regular churchgoers represented only a minority of listeners and viewers of religious programmes and they probably saw little conflict in pursuing both activities. The majority of such listeners and viewers were occasional attenders or non-attenders at church who possibly would not have been in the pews any more frequently had religious broadcasting not been invented, albeit it provided an 'excuse' for avoiding public worship.

A more plausible explanation is that both churchgoing and the audience for religious programmes suffered through the rapid penetration of television, and its associated secular entertainment. In 1950, just 382,000 television licenses were issued, by 1955, it was 4,651,000, and by 1960, 10,554,000. Contemporary surveys and comment all suggested that television ownership negatively impacted church attendance. Thus, in Greater Derby in 1953, 30 per cent of non-television owners worshipped at least monthly compared with 22 per cent of television owners.[87] In December

DOI: 10.1057/9781137512536.0008

1954, Gallup found that owners of television sets were three points less likely than the norm to be frequent churchgoers (22 versus 25 per cent),[88] while in England in December 1963–January 1964 it was reported that 16 per cent of those without a television had worshipped the previous Sunday compared with 10 per cent of all adults.[89] An investigation by Mather and Crowther in England in November 1957 discovered that regular churchgoers, both adults and children, were disproportionately drawn from homes without television. The disparity was most evident on Sunday evenings, when two-thirds of churchgoers came from television-free households.[90] A prominent Free Church writer complained in 1960 that television had diminished congregations, especially on Sunday evenings, and adversely impacted midweek church activities in winter.[91] Such complaints later multiplied with the BBC's Sunday evening repeat of *The Forsyte Saga* in 1968–69. They echo concerns voiced in the interwar period about the effect of Sunday cinema on public worship,[92] which had abated by the long 1950s since cinema admissions peaked in 1946 and, despite a flurry of successful local plebiscites on the Sunday opening of cinemas in 1946–47,[93] they slumped after 1956 – another casualty of television.

Rites of passage

Hitherto we have focused on churchgoing on ordinary Sundays, yet congregations could be swelled by special events in the ecclesiastical calendar, notably Easter (already mentioned in connection with local church censuses), Harvest Festival, Remembrance Sunday, Christmas, and – in the Free Churches – chapel and Sunday school anniversaries. These services attracted the fringe of more irregular worshippers. There were no state occasions which had a similar effect, there being no National Day of Prayer after 1947, and very few other special calls to prayer.[94] Moreover, the 1953 coronation service of Queen Elizabeth II, which certainly did capture the public imagination, was a broadcast experience, 93 per cent telling Gallup afterwards that they had seen all or part of it on television[95] and the BBC estimating the combined television and radio audience at 88 per cent.[96] But the occasional offices of the Churches which continued to have the greatest market penetration were the rites of passage, to celebrate the most significant moments in people's personal lives, which enticed to places of worship, not just those

DOI: 10.1057/9781137512536.0008

immediately affected by the rite, but a wider circle of family and friends who were not accustomed to churchgoing.

Of the individual rites, baptism continued to exert a big pull. Asked by Gallup in February 1957 whether it was right for children to be baptised, 82 per cent of adults replied in the affirmative and a mere 7 per cent in the negative.[97] Of course, the sacrament was widely viewed as a social custom and not often understood in theologically orthodox terms,[98] but the take-up remained impressive. The lion's share of baptisms still went to the Anglicans. Although the most sophisticated analysis of trends (by David Voas), adjusting for neonatal mortality and disputing an apparent peak in 1950, demonstrates a gentle decline throughout most of the 1950s in the proportion of each birth cohort baptised in the Church of England, the majority of babies continued to be so baptised in the early 1960s. Furthermore, it was estimated in 1962 that 62 per cent of the entire English population had been baptised into the Established Church.[99] Roman Catholic infant baptisms grew strongly in England and Wales, by 81 per cent from 72,700 in 1945 to 131,800 in 1963 (or from 11 to 15 per cent of live births),[100] and rather less spectacularly in Scotland, albeit they accounted for a higher proportion of live births there (approaching one-quarter by the early 1960s).[101] Not unexpectedly, a plurality of Scottish babies was baptised into the Church of Scotland, and the majority between 1954 and 1960 (the peak being 54 per cent of births in 1955).[102] Of the Free Churches, the Methodists were the only denomination to count baptisms, and then not until 1961; in the early 1960s they represented just over 5 per cent of live births in England and Wales.[103] Allowing for other religious bodies, it seemed likely to analysts at the time that more than nine-tenths of children continued to be baptised,[104] while a contemporary survey of the Roseworth estate, Stockton-on-Tees, discovered that merely 0.2 per cent of residents were unbaptised.[105] Brierley's retrospective calculations, at ten-yearly intervals, of baptisms as a proportion of live births in the United Kingdom seem rather on the low side (including 74 per cent in 1960).[106]

The other ritual associated with childbirth, the churching of women (a service of purification, blessing, and thanksgiving for the new mother), was less prevalent than it had been. Although an episcopal visitation of the Anglican Diocese of Southwark in 1951 suggested that just over one-half of childbearing women were still being churched, 18 per cent of the diocesan clergy already thought that churching was in decline.[107] According to a study in Bethnal Green in the mid-1950s, maternal influence over young mothers was perhaps the single most important factor in churching's persistence.[108] However, it died out rapidly from the late 1960s, albeit lingering on in small pockets until the 1980s. The churches were somewhat ambivalent about the practice, in any case, especially because of the 'crudest superstitions' popularly associated with the rite,[109] and eventually developed alternative liturgies of thanksgiving for the gift of a child.

Marriage in a place of worship was more pervasive than churching, if not quite as ubiquitous as baptism. Data on the mode of solemnization are only available in England and Wales for four years in the long 1950s (1952, 1957, and 1962–63), although an annual series exists for Scotland. In Britain as a whole 71 per cent of all marriages in the four years were conducted in church, with a period peak of 73 per cent in 1957. In Scotland the mean for the same years was 81 per cent, with the proportion not falling below four-fifths on the annual series until 1962–63 (and with a high of 86 per cent in 1945).[110] The greater religiosity of Scotland over England and Wales, as reflected particularly in church adherence and attendance, doubtless explains this difference. Sample surveys revealed that persons professing no religion were more likely to wed in a register office (Gallup, April 1952)[111] and likewise with non-churchgoers (Odhams Press, September 1947).[112] Other factors may also have influenced the choice of a civil ceremony, such as the greater cost of church marriage and the unwillingness of the Church of England to remarry divorcees (there being a large increase in the incidence of divorce after 1945). The majority of religious marriages (69 per cent in each case) were performed by the Church of England in England and Wales and by the Church of Scotland in Scotland.

Funerals during the long 1950s were universally accompanied by religious rites, with only the rarest exceptions (such as for still-born children). This was confirmed in local studies of Scunthorpe and Rawmarsh in 1954–56 and Billingham in 1957–59 through personal observation, interviews with undertakers, and examination of burial registers.[113] Even at the end of the period, in a study of 359 individuals who had lost a close relative during the five years prior to interview in 1964, only two cases were found of funerals without a religious service. 'In no other area of British life has religion such a near monopoly…death is a religious preserve.'[114] Although this may have reflected the express wishes of the deceased or the bereaved in the overwhelming majority of instances, there can be little doubt that undertakers would generally have arranged

DOI: 10.1057/9781137512536.0008

to provide a minister to officiate at a funeral unless their clients actively chose to 'contract out'. One such minister noted at the time that even those actively hostile to religion, as well as those indifferent to it, were reluctant to challenge the near ubiquity of religious funerals, either from a sense of duty to the departed or a desire to avoid causing distress to bereaved relatives.[115] Moreover, funerals were also great social occasions, as noted by research in the Black Country in 1949: 'Some women make a practice of going to as many funerals as possible. The food is said to be better than at weddings, and funerals are generally bigger affairs.'[116] The popularity of funerals epitomized how, despite falling mortality rates, death remained one of the most important occasions for the expression of familial and neighbourhood solidarity, much as it had been before the Second World War.[117]

Private religious practices

So far, we have considered 'religious behaving' in relation to the varied facets of attendance at places of worship. But religious practice could also take place privately, outside a church context, and sample surveys give us a glimpse into this world, at least as regards the Bible[118] and prayer. A copy of the Bible could be found in the vast majority of British households: 87 per cent in July 1948 (M-O),[119] 90 per cent in February 1954 (Gallup),[120] and 84 per cent in December 1959 (Gallup).[121] The number possessing their own copy was smaller but still significant (56 per cent in Greater Derby in 1953),[122] although hardly anybody would have bought it, most copies being received as gifts from churches, schools, or family members. Reading of the Bible was very much a minority activity, even before allowing for the inflated claims which would surely have been made about the habit. In 1948 the most common answers to M-O's enquiry into the occasions when people used the Bible were: never (21 per cent), at odd times when they felt like it (16 per cent), for reference (14 per cent), and not often (10 per cent); a mere 7 per cent consulted it daily. In February 1954 (Gallup) 23 per cent of Britons admitted to never reading the Bible since leaving school, while in December 1954 (Gallup) 47 per cent had not read it for a very long time, including 14 per cent of frequent and 44 per cent of occasional churchgoers, with 34 per cent reading it during the past fortnight.[123] The Greater Derby survey revealed that men and the under-35s were most likely never to read the Bible

DOI: 10.1057/9781137512536.0008

and the over-55s and middle class to be the most frequent readers. By December 1963–January 1964 regular Bible reading was claimed by just 12 per cent in England (Gallup).[124] Limited familiarity with the Bible was reflected in surveys of knowledge of and attitudes to it. Even an invitation by Gallup to name any of the first four books of the New Testament in October 1949 stumped 25 per cent of respondents (and 30 per cent of those in their twenties).[125] Fewer than one-fifth regarded the Old Testament as literally true, word-for-word, and only one-quarter viewed the New Testament in the same light (Gallup, December 1954, January 1960).[126] Although 72 per cent agreed that the Bible was essential to the survival of the Christian Church (Gallup, January 1960), four-fifths saw no contradiction in stating one could be a Christian without believing all the Bible to be true (Gallup, December 1954, February 1957).[127]

A majority of the population believed in prayer (69 per cent overall, 57 per cent of men, 80 per cent of women, Gallup, January 1950)[128] and that God answered prayer (71 per cent, Gallup, December 1954).[129] Approximately half claimed to pray regularly themselves: 48 per cent in January 1950 (Gallup), 50 per cent in September 1961 (National Opinion Polls),[130] and 43 per cent in December 1963–January 1964 (Gallup),[131] with 44 per cent of readers of *The People* praying daily in January 1951 (including 58 per cent of women and 71 per cent of over-65s) and just 14 per cent never praying.[132] Most (58 per cent) of the same readers said they had taught their own children to say prayers, and 86 per cent of all adults in February 1957 (Gallup) thought it appropriate children generally should be taught to say prayers.[133] However, formal family prayers were said in only 9 per cent of homes in July 1948 (M-O) and grace at mealtimes in 14 per cent. These practices were pursued disproportionately by the over-45s (32 per cent of whom had one or the other, compared with 19 per cent of under-25s).[134]

Notes

1   C.F. Garbett, *The Church of England To-Day* (London: Hodder and Stoughton, 1953), pp. 31, 35–6.
2   R.C. Churchill, *The English Sunday* (London: Watts, 1954), p. 26.
3   *Free Church Directory*, 1965–66, p. 313.
4   W.S.F. Pickering, 'Who Goes to Church?', in C.L. Mitton, ed., *The Social Sciences and the Churches* (Edinburgh: T. & T. Clark, 1972), p. 182.

DOI: 10.1057/9781137512536.0008

5   C.G. Brown, *The Death of Christian Britain: Understanding Secularisation,*
    1800–2000 (2nd edn, London: Routledge, 2009), p. 214; idem, *Religion and*
    Society in Twentieth-Century Britain (Harlow: Pearson, 2006), p. 27.

6   M-O, *Contemporary Churchgoing* (London: M-O, 1949), reprinted from the
    series of articles in *British Weekly*, 13, 20, and 27 January, 3 and 10 February
    1949. M-O failed to interest Victor Gollancz (publishers of *Puzzled People*)
    in producing a book based on the research. Some raw material survives in
    M-OA, notably church observations at 1/2/47/4F, 1/2/47/9B, 1/2/47/9C; and
    documentation on the postal survey at 1/2/47/10A/A1, 1/2/47/10D.

7   *Church Statistics*, 1993, p. 9.

8   L. Paul, *The Deployment and Payment of the Clergy: A Report* (London: Church
    Information Office, 1964), pp. 26, 57, 80, appendix 3.

9   *Methodist Church Statistical Returns*, 1971–74, p. 10.

10 *Rural Methodism: Commission's Report to 1958 Conference* (London: Epworth
    Press, 1958), p. 23.

11 W. Hodgkins, *Sunday: Christian and Social Significance* (London: Independent
    Press, 1960), p. 121.

12 M. McNarney, 'La vie paroissiale', in *Catholicisme anglais* (Paris: Éditions du
    Cerf, 1958), pp. 168–9.

13 A.E.C.W. Spencer (M.E. Daly, ed.), *Arrangements for the Integration of Irish*
    Immigrants in England and Wales (Dublin: Irish Manuscripts Commission,
    2012), p. 100. Spencer's estimate for the proportion making Easter confession
    was almost 40 per cent.

14 G.A. Beck, 'To-Day and To-Morrow', in G.A. Beck, ed., *The English Catholics,*
    1850–1950: Essays to Commemorate the Centenary of the Restoration of the
    Hierarchy of England and Wales (London: Burns Oates, 1950), pp. 586–7.

15 A.E.C.W. Spencer, *The Selection of a Date for the Annual Count of Mass*
    Attendance: A Report (Taunton: Russell-Spencer, 2005), p. 1.

16 A.E.C.W. Spencer, 'The Demography and Sociography of the Roman
    Catholic Community of England and Wales', in L. Bright and S. Clements,
    eds, *The Committed Church* (London: Darton, Longman & Todd, 1966),
    p. 78; idem, *Digest of Statistics of the Catholic Community of England &*
    Wales, 1958–2005, Volume 1: Population and Vital Statistics, Pastoral Services,
    Evangelisation, and Education (Taunton: Russell-Spencer, 2007),
    pp. 75, 81–3.

17 Anon, 'How Many Catholics in England and Wales?' *Catholic Truth*, 6 (1962),
    p. 5; A.E.C.W. Spencer, 'An Evaluation of Roman Catholic Educational Policy
    in England and Wales, 1900–1960', in P. Jebb, ed., *Religious Education: Drift or*
    Decision? (London: Darton, Longman & Todd, 1968), pp. 188, 198.

18 A.E.C.W. Spencer, *Report on the Parish Register, Religious Practice & Population*
    Statistics of the Catholic Church in Scotland, 1967 (Harrow: Pastoral Research
    Centre, 1969), pp. 17–20, 38–43.

DOI: 10.1057/9781137512536.0008

19   Council for Wales and Monmouthshire, *Report on the Welsh Language Today* (House of Commons Papers, Session 1963–64, Cmnd. 2198, London: HMSO, 1963), pp. 80–3.

20   J. Highet, *The Scottish Churches: A Review of Their State 400 Years after the Reformation* (London: Skeffington, 1960), pp. 59–62.

21   M-O, *Contemporary Churchgoing*, p. 14. Twicers still accounted for 19 per cent of Anglican worshippers in Rotherham in 1963; P. Dodd, 'Census of Attendance in Anglican Churches in the County Borough of Rotherham, 1963' (1964), unpublished report in author's possession. A summary is in P. Dodd, 'Who Goes to Church?', *New Society*, 29 April 1965.

22   W.S.F. Pickering, 'The Place of Religion in the Social Structure of Two English Industrial Towns (Rawmasrh, Yorkshire and Scunthorpe, Lincolnshire)' (PhD thesis, University of London, 1958), p. V.18.

23   R. Gill, *The 'Empty' Church Revisited* (Aldershot: Ashgate, 2003), pp. 248–9.

24   Ibid., pp. 232–5.

25   T. Harrisson, *Britain Revisited* (London: Victor Gollancz, 1961), pp. 74, 78. Raw material for the 1960 restudy of religion in Bolton is at M-OA, 1/5/19/64F.

26   X.Y.Z., 'The Redfield United Front Survey', *Redfield Review*, May 1953, pp. 3–5; Dodd, 'Census'.

27   C.D. Field, 'Gradualist or Revolutionary Secularization? A Case Study of Religious Belonging in Inter-War Britain, 1918–1939', *Church History and Religious Culture*, 93 (2013), p. 75.

28   Also for Billingham, although the age categories are not comparable with the other places.

29   E. Moore-Darling, 'Why Villagers Do Not Go to Church', *The Countryman*, 33 (1946), p. 52.

30   P.D. Varney, 'Religion in Rural Norfolk', in D.A. Martin and M. Hill, eds, *A Sociological Yearbook of Religion in Britain*, 3 (London: SCM Press, 1970), pp. 67, 70. It has proved impossible to locate a copy of the 1964 MA thesis on which this essay was based.

31   H.E. Bracey, *English Rural Life* (London: Routledge & Kegan Paul, 1959), pp. 134–7.

32   V.G. Pons, 'The Social Structure of a Hertfordshire Parish' (PhD thesis, University of London, 1955), pp. 197–201.

33   R.E. Pahl, 'Newcomers in Town and Country', in L.M. Munby, ed., *East Anglian Studies* (Cambridge: W. Heffer & Sons, 1968), p. 184.

34   W.M. Williams, *The Sociology of an English Village: Gosforth* (London: Routledge & Kegan Paul, 1956), pp. 178–99; S. Bruce, 'Religion in Gosforth, 1951–2011: A Sociology Classic Revisited', *Rural Theology*, 11 (2013), pp. 39–49.

35   W.M. Williams, *A West Country Village, Ashworthy: Family, Kinship, and Land* (London: Routledge & Kegan Paul, 1963), pp. 7–9, 184–91; S. Bruce, 'Religion

DOI: 10.1057/9781137512536.0008

in Ashworthy, 1958–2011: A Sociology Classic Revisited', *Rural Theology*, 11 (2013), pp. 92–102.

36   I. Cassam, 'Survey of Welsh Religious Life', *Western Mail and South Wales News*, 10–12 January 1952.

37   C. Rosser and C.C. Harris, *The Family and Social Change: A Study of Family and Kinship in a South Wales Town* (London: Routledge & Kegan Paul, 1965), pp. 122, 129.

38   T.M. Owen, 'Chapel and Community in Glan-llyn, Merioneth', in E. Davies and A.D. Rees, eds, *Welsh Rural Communities* (Cardiff: University of Wales Press, 1960), pp. 185–248; Gill, *'Empty' Church*, pp. 38–52 at pp. 44–8; S. Bruce, 'Religion in Rural Wales: Four Restudies', *Contemporary Wales*, 23 (2010), pp. 219–39 at pp. 224–7. Other Welsh rural studies of interest include: R. Frankenberg, *Village on the Border: A Social Study of Religion, Politics, and Football in a North Wales Community* (London: Cohen & West, 1957) – a study of Glyn Ceiriog in 1953; and I. Emmett, *A North Wales Village: A Social Anthropological Study* (London: Routledge & Kegan Paul, 1964) – a study of Llanfrothen Ffestiniog in 1962. It should be noted that the fieldwork for another study, by A.D. Rees, *Life in a Welsh Countryside: A Social Study of Llanfihangel yng Ngwynfa* (Cardiff: University of Wales Press, 1950), pp. 109–30 was conducted during the Second World War.

39   There are also some local sample surveys for the long 1950s, but they are omitted through limitations of space, and because they do not significantly modify conclusions drawn from the national surveys.

40   M-O, *Puzzled People: A Study in Popular Attitudes to Religion, Ethics, Progress, and Politics in a London Borough* (London: Victor Gollancz, 1947), p. 50.

41   K. Bliss, 'Opinion Polls', *Christian News-Letter*, 24 November 1948.

42   M-OA, 1/2/47/10E, 1/2/72/1F (1948), 1/2/72/2E, 1/2/72/3A (1955–56).

43   *News Chronicle*, 1 November 1948; Gallup, *GIPOP*, i., pp. 182, 184.

44   Gallup, *GIPOP*, i., pp. 403–4.

45   *News Chronicle*, 22 May 1958 (for both 1957 and 1958 figures).

46   *Survey of Readership of Newspapers, England and Wales* (London: Gallup Poll, 1952), table 15.

47   Social Surveys (Gallup Poll), *Television and Religion* (London: University of London Press, 1964), pp. 19, 117.

48   *News Review*, 30 October 1947.

49   BBC Audience Research Department, 'Religious Broadcasts and the Public: A Social Survey of the Differences between Non-Listeners and Listeners to Religious Broadcasts' (1955), p. 17, BBC Written Archives Centre, Caversham.

50   *News Chronicle*, 17 April 1957; Gallup, *GIPOP*, i., p. 404.

51   Social Surveys (Gallup Poll), *Television and Religion*, pp. 58, 128–9.

DOI: 10.1057/9781137512536.0008

52 C.D. Field, '*Puzzled People* Revisited: Religious Believing and Belonging in Wartime Britain, 1939-45', *Twentieth Century British History*, 19 (2008), p. 462; idem, 'Gradualist or Revolutionary Secularization?', p. 75.

53 Christian Economic and Social Research Foundation, *Setting Up a Home* (London: the Foundation, 1957), pp. 10–15 and *Aspects of the Problem Facing the Churches* (London: the Foundation, 1960), passim. This was a study of young wives in Birmingham, Leeds, and London.

54 B.E. Shenfield, *Social Policies for Old Age: A Review of Social Provision for Old Age in Great Britain* (London: Routledge and Kegan Paul, 1957), p. 229.

55 R.J. Havighurst, 'Life beyond Family and Work', in E.W. Burgess, ed., *Aging in Western Societies* (Chicago: University of Chicago Press, 1960), p. 332.

56 P. Callard, 'The Church and Older People', *Social Service Quarterly*, 33 (1959–60), p. 115.

57 I.M. Richardson, *Age and Need: A Study of Older People in North-East Scotland* (Edinburgh: E. & S. Livingstone, 1964), pp. 89–91.

58 P. Townsend and S. Tunstall, 'Isolation, Desolation, and Loneliness', in E. Shanas, P. Townsend, D. Wedderburn, H. Friis, P. Milhøj, and J. Stehouwer, *Old People in Three Industrial Societies* (London: Routledge and Kegan Paul, 1968), pp. 269–70.

59 M.A. Abrams, *The Teenage Consumer* (London: London Press Exchange, 1959), p. 17.

60 B.H. Reed, *Eighty Thousand Adolescents: A Study of Young People in the City of Birmingham* (London: Allen & Unwin, 1950), pp. 28–9, 42.

61 M.G. Schofield, *The Sexual Behaviour of Young People* (London: Longmans, 1965), pp. 148, 236.

62 The interaction of churchgoing, class, and radicalism in this February 1957 Gallup poll is explored by R. Stark, 'Class, Radicalism, and Religious Involvement in Great Britain', *American Sociological Review*, 29 (1964), pp. 698–706; and C.Y. Glock and R. Stark, *Religion and Society in Tension* (Chicago: Rand McNally, 1965), pp. 193–9.

63 J.M. Mogey, *Family and Neighbourhood: Two Studies in Oxford* (London: Oxford University Press, 1956), p. 147.

64 H. Jennings, *Societies in the Making: A Study of Development and Redevelopment within a County Borough* (London: Routledge & Kegan Paul, 1962), p. 254.

65 J.B. Mays, 'New Hope in Newtown', *New Society*, 22 August 1963.

66 C.D. Field, 'Faith in the Metropolis: Opinion Polls and Christianity in Post-War London', *London Journal*, 24 (1999), pp. 72–5; unpublished material supplied by the late D.V. Glass to the author.

67 P. Willmott and M. Young, *Family and Class in a London Suburb* (London: Routledge & Kegan Paul, 1960), p. 93 – a study of Woodford; P. Willmott,

DOI: 10.1057/9781137512536.0008

The Evolution of a Community: A Study of Dagenham After Forty Years (London: Routledge & Kegan Paul, 1963), p. 140.

68   D.H.E. Butler and D.E. Stokes, *Political Change in Britain: The Evolution of Electoral Choice* (2nd edn, London: Macmillan, 1974), p. 157.

69   For an introduction to religious broadcasting in the period, see M. Dinwiddie, *Religion by Radio: Its Place in British Broadcasting* (London: George Allen & Unwin, 1968); K.M. Wolfe, *The Churches and the British Broadcasting Corporation, 1922–1956: The Politics of Broadcast Religion* (London: SCM Press, 1984), pp. 313–537; B. Sendall, J. Potter, and P. Bonner, *Independent Television in Britain* (6 vols, London: Macmillan, 1982–2003), i., pp. 103–4, 279–83, 360–3, ii., pp. 288–93.

70   Field, 'Gradualist or Revolutionary Secularization?', pp. 69–71.

71   *News Review*, 6 November 1947.

72   Social Surveys (Gallup Poll), *Television and Religion*, pp. 97, 131–2.

73   Unpublished table in author's possession.

74   Social Surveys (Gallup Poll), *Television and Religion*, pp. 127–8.

75   F. House, 'Review of the Aims and Achievements of Religious Broadcasting, 1923–1948', pp. 12–14. Copy in M-OA, 1/2/47/12E.

76   M-O, 'Notes on Projected Survey on Religious Broadcasting', 4 May 1949, M-OA, 1/2/47/12E.

77   BBC Audience Research Department, 'Religious Broadcasts and the Public', especially pp. 3–12, 20–3. Although technically unpublished, copies of this report have found their way into several research libraries – see COPAC. It is summarized in R.J.E. Silvey, 'The Audiences for Religious Broadcasts', in *Religion on the Air: Three Talks Given to the St Paul's Lecture Society* (London: British Broadcasting Corporation, 1956), pp. 5–14; A. Briggs, *The History of Broadcasting in the United Kingdom, Volume IV: Sound and Vision* (Oxford: Oxford University Press, 1979), pp. 796–800; and Wolfe, *Churches and the British Broadcasting Corporation*, pp. 470–4.

78   T. Cauter and J. Downham, *The Communication of Ideas: A Study of Contemporary Influences on Urban Life* (London: Chatto & Windus, 1954), pp. 56–9.

79   Gallup, *GIPOP*, i., p. 404.

80   *News Review*, 6 November 1947.

81   Social Surveys (Gallup Poll), *Television and Religion*, pp. 95–6, 131.

82   Independent Television Authority, *Religious Programmes on Independent Television* (London: the Authority, 1962), pp. 13–15, 51–6.

83   R. Currie, A.D. Gilbert, and L. Horsley, *Churches and Churchgoers: Patterns of Church Growth in the British Isles since 1700* (Oxford: Clarendon Press, 1977), pp. 235–6.

84   House, 'Review', pp. 9–12; *Manchester Guardian*, 10 September 1952.

85   T. Barnes, *Songs of Praise: Celebrating 50 Years* (Oxford: Lion, 2011).

DOI: 10.1057/9781137512536.0008

86 Currie et al., *Churches*, pp. 235–7; Independent Television Authority, *Religious Programmes*, p. 53.

87 Cauter and Downham, *Communication of Ideas*, p. 157.

88 BBC Audience Research Department, 'Religious Broadcasts and the Public', pp. 15–16.

89 Social Surveys (Gallup Poll), *Television and Religion*, p. 20.

90 *Sunday Times*, 13, 27 April, 4 May 1958.

91 Hodgkins, *Sunday*, p. 133.

92 Field, 'Gradualist or Revolutionary Secularization?', pp. 68–9.

93 Including Liverpool in May 1947, where 61 per cent of electors voted in favour; *The Times*, 22 May 1947.

94 P. Williamson, 'National Days of Prayer: The Churches, the State, and Public Worship in Britain, 1899–1957', *English Historical Review*, 128 (2013), pp. 327, 358–63.

95 Gallup, *GIPOP*, i., p. 300.

96 P. Ziegler, *Crown and People* (London: Collins, 1978), p. 114.

97 Gallup, *GIPOP*, i., p. 407.

98 D. Clark, *Between Pulpit and Pew: Folk Religion in a North Yorkshire Fishing Village* (Cambridge: Cambridge University Press, 1982), pp. 115–19; R.P.M. Sykes, 'Popular Religion in Dudley and the Gornals, *c.* 1914–1965' (PhD thesis, University of Wolverhampton, 1999), pp. 96–101, 176–80.

99 R.F. Neuss, *Facts and Figures about the Church of England, Number 3* (London: Church Information Office, 1965), pp. 54, 58; Currie et al., *Churches*, pp. 167–8; D. Voas, 'Intermarriage and the Demography of Secularization', *British Journal of Sociology*, 54 (2003), pp. 83–108.

100 Taunton, Pastoral Research Centre Trust Archives, A.E.C.W. Spencer, 'Work Done by the Newman Demographic Survey on the Revision of Baptismal Statistics' (1958) and idem, 'Report to the Catholic Clergy of England & Wales on the Parish Register Returns for 1961' (1962); Spencer, *Digest*, p. 35.

101 J. Darragh, 'The Catholic Population of Scotland, 1878–1977', in D. McRoberts, ed., *Modern Scottish Catholicism, 1878–1978* (Glasgow: Burns, 1979), p. 231.

102 Currie et al., *Churches*, p. 170.

103 B.E. Jones, 'Another Decade of Methodism: Facts and Figures about British Methodism, with Special Reference to the Sixties (1960–70)' (1971), pp. 13–15, unpublished report in author's possession.

104 For example, W.S.F. Pickering, 'The Present Position of the Anglican and Methodist Churches in the Light of Available Statistics', in W.S.F. Pickering, ed., *Anglican-Methodist Relations: Some Institutional Factors* (London: Darton, Longman & Todd, 1961), p. 11; P.R. Kaim-Caudle, *Religion in Billingham, 1957–59* (Billingham-on-Tees: Billingham Community Association, 1962),

DOI: 10.1057/9781137512536.0008

pp. 3–4. Cf. W.S.F. Pickering, 'The Persistence of Rites of Passage: Towards an Explanation', *British Journal of Sociology*, 25 (1974), pp. 63–4.

105   Paul, *Deployment*, pp. 28, 287.

106   P.W. Brierley, *A Century of British Christianity: Historical Statistics, 1900–1985* (Bromley: MARC Europe, 1989), pp. 37, 39; idem, *Religion in Britain, 1900 to 2000* (London: Christian Research, 1998), p. 10; idem, 'Religion', in A.H. Halsey and J. Webb, eds, *Twentieth-Century British Social Trends* (Basingstoke: Macmillan, 2000), pp. 664–5; idem, ed., *UK Christian Handbook, Religious Trends, No. 3, 2002/2003* (London: Christian Research, 2001), p. 2.2.

107   M. Houlbrooke, *Rite out of Time: A Study of the Ancient Rite of Churching and its Survival in the Twentieth Century* (Donington: Shaun Tyas, 2011), pp. 50, 71–100, 126.

108   M. Young and P. Willmott, *Family and Kinship in East London* (London: Routledge & Kegan Paul, 1957), pp. 39–40.

109   S.H. Mayor, 'The Religion of the British People', *Hibbert Journal*, 49 (1960-61), p. 42. Cf. Clark, *Between Pulpit and Pew*, pp. 119, 122–4; Sykes, 'Popular Religion', pp. 180–5, 328–31.

110   Currie et al., *Churches*, pp. 224, 228–9.

111   Unpublished report in author's possession.

112   *News Review*, 30 October 1947.

113   Pickering, 'Present Position', pp. 17–18; idem, 'Persistence', pp. 68–9; Kaim-Caudle, *Religion in Billingham*, pp. 3–4; P.R. Kaim-Caudle, 'Church & Social Change: A Study of Religion in Billingham, 1959-66', *New Christian*, 9 March 1967.

114   G.E.S. Gorer, *Death, Grief, and Mourning in Contemporary Britain* (London: Cresset Press, 1965), p. 30.

115   Mayor, 'Religion of the British People', p. 41.

116   D. Rich, 'Spare Time in the Black Country', in L. Kuper, ed., *Living in Towns* (London: Cresset Press, 1953), p. 332.

117   E. Roberts, 'The Lancashire Way of Death', in R. Houlbrooke, ed., *Death, Ritual, and Bereavement* (London: Routledge, 1989), pp. 188–207.

118   For background, see C.D. Field, 'Is the Bible Becoming a Closed Book? British Opinion Poll Evidence', *Journal of Contemporary Religion*, 29 (2014), pp. 503–28.

119   *Daily Graphic*, 10 August 1948; M-OA, 1/2/47/12C.

120   *News Chronicle*, 8 March 1954; Gallup, *GIPOP*, i., pp. 316–17.

121   *Gallup Political & Economic Index*, 371 (1991), p. 51.

122   Cauter and Downham, *Communication of Ideas*, pp. 57–9.

123   BBC Audience Research Department, 'Religious Broadcasts', pp. 34–6.

124   Social Surveys (Gallup Poll), *Television and Religion*, pp. 29–30, 131.

DOI: 10.1057/9781137512536.0008

125 *News Chronicle*, 3 January 1950, followed up in the correspondence columns on 4–6 and 10 January 1950; Gallup, *GIPOP*, i., p. 210.

126 *Gallup Political Index*, 225 (1979), p. 15.

127 *News Chronicle*, 15 April 1957; Gallup, *GIPOP*, i., p. 405.

128 *News Chronicle*, 9 February 1950; Gallup, *GIPOP*, i., p. 218.

129 BBC Audience Research Department, 'Religious Broadcasts', pp. 36–7.

130 Unpublished report in author's possession.

131 Social Surveys (Gallup Poll), *Television and Religion*, pp. 27–9, 131.

132 G.E.S. Gorer, *Exploring English Character* (London: Cresset Press, 1955), pp. 452–3.

133 Gallup, *GIPOP*, i., p. 407.

134 M-OA, 1/2/47/12C.

DOI: 10.1057/9781137512536.0008

4
Believing

Abstract: *The availability of opinion polls means that, for the first time in the 1950s, it is possible to probe popular beliefs in a quantitatively representative rather than anecdotal fashion. Four dimensions of belief are considered, starting with orthodox and heterodox beliefs, broadly equating to those which contemporary Churches and clergy would have understood as, respectively, falling within and outside of the framework of traditional Christianity. Beliefs in God, an afterlife, astrology, and superstitions are among those discussed. Attitudes to a range of religion-related public issues (such as the Churches, Sabbatarianism, Catholics, and Jews) are then considered, followed by an analysis by religious variables of attitudes to more secular topics (including moral questions such as divorce and capital punishment and investigation of religion and voting behaviour).*

Keywords: heterodox beliefs; moral questions; religious attitudes; religious beliefs; Sunday observance; voting preference

Field, Clive D. *Britain's Last Religious Revival? Quantifying Belonging, Behaving, and Believing in the Long 1950s.* Basingstoke: Palgrave Macmillan, 2015. DOI: 10.1057/9781137512536.0009.

Orthodox beliefs

The development of the sample survey made it possible to investigate the extent of religious believing representatively rather than anecdotally. The territory was first explored in detail by M-O in the London borough of Hammersmith in 1944–45 and reported in *Puzzled People* (1947), whose title encapsulated the apparent confusion, inconsistency, and superficiality which often characterized popular belief – 'the great muddle', as M-O described it, or 'a mental and moral chaos', in the words of the Ethical Union, which sponsored the investigation.[1] The study was replicated in 1960, evidently revealing similar contradictions (such as the many disbelievers in God who prayed, went to church, and believed in life after death and the divinity of Christ). Regrettably, only one table from the replication seems ever to have been published, and no original documentation has been traced.[2] The emphasis here, therefore, is necessarily on unitary measures of religious belief.[3]

Perhaps the most basic indicator was belief in God,[4] but its extent varied according to question-formulation, as M-O discovered when it ran a controlled experiment on two identical samples of working-class women, one being offered a 'haven't you made up your mind?' option and one not.[5] The former version was deemed to yield better results and asked by M-O in a survey of 11 areas (mostly in England) in 1947, with 77 per cent of interviewees believing in God, 7 per cent disbelieving, and 16 per cent uncertain. Believers were most prevalent among women (84 per cent) and the over-40s (82 per cent), disbelievers among men and under-25s (both 10 per cent).[6] A trio of Gallup polls in Britain (Table 4.1) indicated some decline in belief in God throughout the long 1950s, from 84 per cent in December 1947 to 78 per cent in February 1957 to 71 per cent in March–April 1963,[7] with a subset of belief in a personal God falling from 45 to 41 to 38 per cent (the remainder believing in some sort of spirit or vital force that controlled life). Aggregate belief in 1947 was comparable with other Western European nations apart from France (66 per cent) but less than in the United States (94 per cent), Canada (95 per cent), and Australia (95 per cent). National Opinion Polls in September 1961 recorded higher figures for believers in God (91 per cent, including 6 per cent who said probably and 23 per cent who had experienced a period of disbelief) and the sub-set of believers in a personal God (57 per cent).[8] The discrepancy with Gallup's findings is perhaps explained by variant question-wording and methodology.

DOI: 10.1057/9781137512536.0009

The large-scale survey by David Glass in the Associated Rediffusion Area in 1960 returned 85 per cent belief in God, with 78 per cent for men and 91 per cent for women, but no difference between non-manual and manual occupations. The figure reached 96 per cent for Catholics, but even 25 per cent of those professing no religion counted themselves among the believers.[9]

Belief in life after death was less pervasive than belief in God. It was first measured, by Gallup, in March 1939, when it stood at 48 per cent.[10] The figure remained virtually unchanged in December 1947 (Table 4.2), at 49 per cent, which was joint lowest (with Sweden) of 12 countries

TABLE 4.1   *Belief in God, Great Britain, 1947–63 (percentages down)*

	12/1947	2/1957	3–4/1963
N	2,000	2,261	1,076
Believe in personal God	45	41	38
Believe in some sort of spirit/vital force	39	37	33
Disbelieve/don't know	16	22	29

Sources: 12/1947 = *News Chronicle*, 13 January 1948, G.H. Gallup, ed., *The Gallup International Public Opinion Polls: Great Britain, 1937–1975 [GIPOP]* (2 vols, New York: Random House, 1976), i., p. 166; 2/1957 = *News Chronicle*, 15, 17 April 1957, Gallup, *GIPOP*, i., p. 405; 3–4/1963 = *Gallup Political Index*, 39 (1963), p. 75, B. Martin, 'Comments on Some Gallup Poll Statistics', in D.A. Martin, ed., *A Sociological Yearbook of Religion in Britain [1]* (London: SCM Press, 1968), pp. 151–3, 178, Gallup, *GIPOP*, i., p. 682.

TABLE 4.2   *Belief in life after death, Great Britain, 1947–63 (percentages down)*

	12/1947	2/1957	3/1960	3–4/1963
N	2,000	2,261	1,000	1,076
Believe	49	54	56	53
Disbelieve	27	17	18	22
Don't know	24	29	26	25

Sources: 12/1947 = *News Chronicle*, 13 January 1948, H.J. Eysenck, *The Psychology of Politics* (London: Routledge & Kegan Paul, 1954), p. 33, Gallup, *GIPOP*, i., p. 166; 2/1957 = *News Chronicle*, 15 April 1957, R. Stark, 'Class, Radicalism, and Religious Involvement in Great Britain', *American Sociological Review*, 29 (1964), pp. 705–6, C.Y. Glock and R. Stark, *Religion and Society in Tension* (Chicago: Rand McNally, 1965), pp. 198–9, Gallup, *GIPOP*, i., p. 405; 3/1960 = P. Alan, 'The Statistics of Belief', *The Humanist*, 76 (1961), pp. 169–71; 3–4/1963 = *Gallup Political Index*, 39 (1963), p. 75, B. Martin, 'Comments on Some Gallup Poll Statistics', in D.A. Martin, ed., *A Sociological Yearbook of Religion in Britain [1]* (London: SCM Press, 1968), pp. 154–5, 179, Gallup, *GIPOP*, i., p. 682.

DOI: 10.1057/9781137512536.0009

surveyed, Canada recording the highest (78 per cent). Asked to define the nature of the afterlife, British believers sub-divided into 21 per cent who spoke of the spirit living on, 7 per cent of heaven and hell, 3 per cent of reincarnation, with 5 per cent giving other replies and 13 per cent having no idea. Belief in an afterlife minimally strengthened in the 1950s, according to Gallup (Table 4.2), to 54 per cent in February 1957, 56 per cent in March 1960, and 53 per cent in March–April 1963.[11] Disbelievers, who had numbered 27 per cent in 1947 fell to 17 per cent in 1957 and 18 per cent in 1960, with one-quarter in all years expressing uncertainty. Among readers of *The People* in 1951, 47 per cent believed in an afterlife and 22 per cent not.[12] All studies revealed belief to be stronger among women (62 per cent in 1960) than among men and in the older than in the younger age cohorts, while in a new suburb of Gloucester in 1961 even 14 per cent of churchgoers thought there was nothing beyond death and 22 per cent were unsure.[13]

A plurality of Britons (43 per cent) in December 1954 (Gallup) was convinced that lifetime behaviour affected destiny after death,[14] but only 18 per cent of readers of *The People* in 1951 believed in hell.[15] Among believers in God in September 1961 (National Opinion Polls) 26 per cent also believed in hell, although just 6 per cent thought disbelievers in God were automatically destined for hell.[16] About one-third of adults believed in the devil in February 1957 (Gallup),[17] September 1961 (National Opinion Polls), and March–April 1963 (Gallup).[18] Gallup recorded disbelievers in the devil at 42 and 47 per cent, respectively, albeit National Opinion Polls returned 56 per cent and *The People* 60 per cent (including 67 per cent of men).[19] Belief in Jesus remained high (at around four-fifths), but the proportion holding that He was the Son of God declined in Gallup polls from 71 per cent in February 1957[20] to 59 per cent in March—April 1963,[21] with those saying He was just a man or a story increasing from 15 to 23 per cent. Belief in Jesus as the Son of God in 1963 was highest for Catholics (85 per cent) and lowest among men (46 per cent against 71 per cent of women).

Heterodox beliefs

Into this melting pot of at least nominally Christian orthodoxy was stirred a variety of alternative belief systems. M-O tried to get to grips with some of them in its report on 'Common beliefs, superstitions, and folklore'

DOI: 10.1057/9781137512536.0009

in December 1948, based on interviews with 125 men and women.[22] Astrology seems to have enjoyed a post-war resurgence, following a wartime decline from 1941, perhaps linked to a fresh set of uncertainties about the post-1945 future over reconstruction, economic austerity, and new international tensions.[23] Although admitted belief in astrology was relatively low (22 per cent according to a national survey by M-O in 1947, with an additional 20 per cent undecided or refusing to say),[24] people's behaviour told a different story. Annual sales of *Old Moore's Almanack* were conservatively estimated at 5,000,000 copies in 1947, one for every other household,[25] and readership of horoscopes in newspapers or magazines was vast, 71 per cent consulting them regularly or occasionally in January 1951 (Odhams Press), albeit 76 per cent never heeded their advice and 60 per cent thought there was nothing in them. Women (53 per cent) were much more likely to read them regularly than men (30 per cent).[26] One-fifth of adults believed in foretelling the future by various means (Gallup, March 1951),[27] and 28 per cent had been to a fortune-teller, half of them more than once (Odhams Press, January 1951).[28]

Two-fifths of Britons (Gallup, September 1949) believed in telepathy,[29] and two-thirds of M-O's middle-class panel, 43 per cent of the latter claiming personal experience of it.[30] One in seven in February 1957 believed it possible to exchange messages with the dead,[31] much the same as in a previous Gallup enquiry in March 1940,[32] with one-third ambivalent. One in ten, disproportionately women, believed in ghosts (Gallup, March 1950).[33] Finally, there were superstitions, believed in by 35 per cent of Britons in May 1946 (Gallup), including 48 per cent of women (double the proportion of men) and 45 per cent of those in their 20s (against one-third of the over-30s). Behaviour sometimes contradicted belief for, in the same study, as many as 35 per cent admitted to throwing salt over their shoulder (including 47 per cent of women), 41 per cent to touching wood (53 per cent of women), and 53 per cent to avoiding walking under ladders (61 per cent of women).[34] Fourteen years later, in Sheffield in 1960, 77 per cent of individuals (among them several clergy) were seen deliberately walking around a ladder positioned over a pavement, even when it was not safe to do so, rather than pass underneath it.[35] Of course, 'belief' was often half-hearted; as M-O commented, 'People typically say they observe superstitions as a sort of personal indemnity against anything which may follow non-observance.'[36] In January 1951 (Odhams Press) 12 per cent had a lucky mascot and 9 per cent an especially lucky day.[37]

DOI: 10.1057/9781137512536.0009

Attitudes to religious issues

This rich tapestry of popular religious belief extended into religious attitudes, also, which could be full of contradiction. Whereas three-fifths of Greater Londoners in 1960 claimed religion played a very or rather important part in their lives (53 per cent of men and 68 per cent of women),[38] only 28 per cent of Britons in March 1963 (Gallup) described themselves as religious.[39] While 69 per cent proclaimed the importance of fighting to preserve freedom of religion in June 1955 (Gallup),[40] by September 1963 (Gallup) freedom of religion was ranked the least significant of four liberties, scoring just 8 per cent against 38 per cent for freedom from want and 37 per cent for freedom from fear.[41] Greater economic security (48 per cent) trumped more religion (36 per cent) as the world's greater priority in a Gallup poll in February 1957.[42] Likewise, in April 1955 (Gallup) religion meant far less to respondents (20 per cent) than work (44 per cent) or hobbies (31 per cent),[43] and in England in December 1963–January 1964 (Gallup) they were far more likely to be influenced by the opinions of others (65 per cent) than religion (19 per cent).[44] Only when compared with politics, for which most people had relatively little time, did religion fare better, but the majority in June 1948[45] and plurality in February 1957[46] still viewed politics as the more influential in shaping everyday life (Gallup).

In fact, Britons could be somewhat critical of organized religion,[47] three-fifths in February 1947 (Gallup) either denying that it had a mission to fulfil in contemporary Britain or thinking it was failing in that mission.[48] Just 21 per cent in July 1948 (M-O) reckoned the Churches were succeeding in their work, 52 per cent saying they were failing and 15 per cent indifferent.[49] Respondents to the Odhams Press survey in September 1947 were more charitable, 27 per cent assessing the Churches were carrying out their job badly, 50 per cent fairly well, and 21 per cent well.[50] Approximately one-quarter in Britain-wide Gallup polls regarded religion as old-fashioned and out-of-date (February 1957,[51] 45 per cent in England alone in December 1963–January 1964)[52] and as incompatible with science (February 1958).[53] A majority (52 per cent in Britain in February 1957,[54] 62 per cent in England in December 1963–January 1964),[55] according to Gallup, said religion was losing its influence over national life. A mere 14 per cent in January 1963 (Gallup) thought the Churches had great influence on the country's future (with a high of 19 per cent for the over-65s), 31 per cent conceding they had

DOI: 10.1057/9781137512536.0009

some influence, but 45 per cent saying they had little or none (peaking at 55 per cent of the upper and upper-middle classes and 53 per cent among those aged 35–44).[56] While the clergy were still generally well regarded, they were seen in one survey as less useful than doctors, police, grocers, atomic research scientists, and MPs (M-O, summer 1960),[57] and in another as often slow to accept new ideas and not overworked.[58] In June–July 1959 (Research Services) religious figures came well down the list of most admired individuals, after politicians, royalty, entertainers, cultural figures, sportspeople, and military leaders.[59]

Ecclesiastical interventions on the political stage were likewise generally unpopular, Gallup reporting 72 per cent agreement in May 1956 that prominent leaders such as the Archbishop of Canterbury should 'keep right out of politics'.[60] The reduction to 53 per cent in another Gallup poll in February 1957 reflected the fact that the question was about the Churches speaking out on social as well as political issues.[61] Support for separating Church and state was also exemplified by a plurality in November 1955 (*Daily Express* Poll)[62] and February 1957 (Gallup)[63] endorsing disestablishment of the Church of England.[64]

However, by virtue of legislation, religion and politics could not be kept in entirely distinct compartments. Religious education in state schools was a case in point, following the Education Act 1944. More than two-thirds of adults in Gallup studies in November 1951[65] and December 1954[66] emphasized the importance of providing it, with only a minority demand for teaching about world religions besides Christianity (February 1957,[67] December 1963–January 1964).[68] Even as late as January–February 1963 (British Market Research Bureau), 83 per cent considered a religious background in children's education to be important.[69] There was more division about public funding of church schools, albeit approval ran at 49 per cent in November 1951 (Gallup)[70] and one-third backed an increase in state grants to such schools in May 1959 (Gallup).[71]

Sunday observance was another area where law and religion were intertwined.[72] Brown's portrayal of the late 1940s and 1950s emphasizes their 'puritan climate', but this was not entirely true of Sundays, which growing numbers wished to see 'brightened up' and statutory restrictions relaxed. The campaign to do so was led by pressure groups such as the Brighter Sunday Association (formed in 1949 and renamed the Sunday Freedom Association in 1950) and the Better Sunday Society (1958) – and fiercely resisted by the Lord's Day Observance Society (LDOS).[73] It culminated in 1961 in the appointment of a Departmental Committee

DOI: 10.1057/9781137512536.0009

on the Law on Sunday Observance which, chaired by Lord Crathorne, reported in 1964 and recommended significant deregulation.[74] The committee substituted for a Royal Commission on the subject, for which – following the defeat of John Parker's Sunday Observance Bill in January 1953 – there had been calls, backed by 56 per cent of the public (Gallup, May 1958).[75] This grass-roots appetite for reform had surfaced in M-O's 1949 book, which portrayed Sunday as 'a day of negatives and emptiness', largely stripped of its religious character but yet to acquire the full attributes of a non-religious festival.[76] It was further illuminated in opinion polls,[77] with 47 per cent by May 1958 (Gallup) wanting to see Sundays treated like any other day so far as the law was concerned.[78] Even one-quarter of churchgoers agreed with the proposition, confirming evidence from local surveys in 1956 showing Protestants combining public worship with an array of secular activities on Sundays.[79] A study by National Opinion Polls of professing Anglicans in 1960 likewise found no significant differences between churchgoers and non-churchgoers in the way in which they spent the Sabbath.[80]

According to the national polls (by Gallup, unless otherwise stated), popular demand for liberalization varied somewhat dependent upon specific facets of Sunday observance. Temperance-based Sabbatarianism was rapidly ceasing to be acceptable. Two-thirds of Britons supported the Sunday opening of public houses and other licensed premises in July 1959,[81] and in May 1958 two-fifths wanted the law changed to permit them to open the same hours on Sundays as weekdays. Wales (including Monmouthshire) was a special case since, largely as a result of the strength of Welsh Nonconformity, licensed premises had been prohibited from opening under the Sunday Closing (Wales) Act 1881 until it was repealed by the Licensing Act 1961, which provided for local authorities to hold referenda on the subject at septennial intervals. In the first such referendum, on 8 November 1961, 47 per cent of the Welsh electorate turned out, of whom 54 per cent voted 'wet' and 46 per cent 'dry'. There were 'wet' majorities in all four county boroughs (Cardiff, Merthyr Tydfil, Newport, and Swansea) and five of the 13 counties (Brecon, Flint, Glamorgan, Monmouth, and Radnor), by a resounding margin in all instances apart from Brecon and Radnor.[82] The case for Sunday opening had been strongly advanced by the Seven Day Opening Council (representing licensed victuallers and brewing interests) and opposed by the United Council on Alcohol, the Fellowship of the Lord's Day in Wales, and the Welsh temperance movement.

DOI: 10.1057/9781137512536.0009

One-half of Britons desired places of entertainment, such as theatres, to be allowed to open on Sundays as on weekdays in January 1953, February 1957, and May 1958 (Table 4.3), while 57 per cent in May 1958 disagreed with the LDOS in forcing the Bishop of Coventry to cancel a ballet performance he had arranged for a Sunday.[83] Three-fifths approved of games being played on Sundays in September–October 1948 (M-O),[84] and 43–47 per cent favoured professional sport on Sundays in 1953, 1957, and 1958 (Table 4.3). Fewer (just over one-quarter) endorsed horse-racing on Sundays, with three-fifths opposed, possibly on anti-gambling grounds, since horse-racing implied on- and off-course betting (Table 4.3). The campaign to ease Sunday trading laws had not yet begun in earnest, but it is notable that 67 per cent in April 1962 did not think it wrong to buy things on Sundays.[85]

Finally, in terms of public attitudes to religion, mention should be made of the incidence of religious prejudice as documented (mostly) in Gallup polls. Churchgoers generally were on the receiving end of some of this, especially for their aversion to change, and most adults were unconvinced that worshippers led better or happier lives than anybody else (December 1954,[86] December 1963–January 1964[87]). This was partly self-justificatory, the public arguing overwhelmingly that it was unnecessary

TABLE 4.3   *Attitudes to the deregulation of Sunday activities, Great Britain, 1953–58 (percentages down)*

	1/1953	2/1957	5/1958
N	2,000	2,261	1,000
Places of entertainment			
Approve	50	55	50
Disapprove	41	39	39
Don't know	9	6	11
Professional sport			
Approve	43	47	46
Disapprove	48	45	41
Don't know	9	8	13
Horse racing			
Approve	26	29	NA
Disapprove	64	62	NA
Don't know	10	9	NA

Sources: 1/1953 = *News Chronicle*, 31 January 1953, Gallup, *GIPOP*, i., p. 319; 2/1957 = *News Chronicle*, 16 April 1957, Gallup, *GIPOP*, i., p. 407; 5/1958 = *News Chronicle*, 22 May 1958, Home Office, *Report of the Departmental Committee on the Law on Sunday Observance* (House of Commons Papers, Session 1964–65, Cmnd. 2528, London: HMSO, 1964), p. 71, Gallup, *GIPOP*, i., pp. 466–7.

DOI: 10.1057/9781137512536.0009

to go to church to be a Christian (85 per cent in February 1957)[88] or to lead a good and useful life (95 per cent in December 1963–January 1964).[89] There was some suspicion of religious 'enthusiasm', exemplified in opposition to or disinterest in Billy Graham's crusade expressed by two-fifths in March and May 1954.[90] Even the Salvation Army was not above criticism, as M-O discovered in its study in London, Bristol, and Preston in 1946, 14 per cent of respondents finding some fault with it, especially among the young.[91] On the other hand, Gallup also recorded some animosity toward atheists, they being, respectively in November 1958[92] and December 1963–January 1964,[93] the least desirable prospective MP and neighbour of any religious group mentioned.

There were also lingering manifestations of anti-Catholicism[94] and anti-Semitism.[95] The former was described by a Congregational minister of the time thus: 'The Englishman is still a natural Protestant. Militant antipathy to the Roman Catholic Church is largely a spent force, but in English society that Church still seems to many people something alien. Most agnostics are at least Protestant agnostics...'[96] One person in three in August 1959 felt that Catholics had more power in the country than they should,[97] 17 per cent expressed a dislike for their creed in February 1957,[98] 13 per cent entertained a poor opinion of them in December 1961,[99] and in November 1958 16 per cent were disinclined to vote for a Catholic candidate at a parliamentary election.[100] As Table 4.4 shows, support

TABLE 4.4   *Attitudes to Church unity negotiations, Great Britain, 1949–63 (percentages down)*

	11/1949	2/1957	10/1961	6-7/1963
N	2,000	2,261	1,000	1,072
Anglican/Nonconformist unity				
Approve	45	49	54	61
Disapprove	19	14	15	10
Neither/don't mind	24	NA	18	12
Don't know	12	37	13	17
Catholic/Protestant unity				
Approve	23	NA	40	53
Disapprove	48	NA	33	18
Neither/don't mind	17	NA	15	10
Don't know	12	NA	12	19

Sources: 11/1949 = Gallup, *GIPOP*, i., p. 216; 2/1957 = ibid., pp. 406–7; 10/1961 = *Gallup Political Index*, 23 (1961), p. 44, *Catholic Herald*, 12 January 1962, Gallup, *GIPOP*, i., pp. 606–7; 6–7/1963 = *Gallup Political Index*, 42 (1963), p. 129, *Sunday Telegraph*, 14 July 1963, Gallup, *GIPOP*, i., p. 697.

DOI: 10.1057/9781137512536.0009

for Catholic/Protestant church unity was lower than for Anglican/ Nonconformist unity, although the gap closed from 22 per cent in November 1949 to 14 per cent in October 1961 and 8 per cent in June–July 1963, and the proportion in favour of Catholic/Protestant unity rose from 23 per cent in 1949 to 53 per cent in 1963. Similarly positive was majority support for the efforts of Popes John XXIII and Paul VI, at the height of the Cold War, to defuse East-West tensions and for the establishment of official relationships between the Vatican and Kremlin (Gallup, October 1961, April and June–July 1963).[101] The Catholic Church also enjoyed a reputation for being relatively free of class bias (Gallup, December 1963–January 1964).[102]

Anti-Semitism apparently grew in the immediate post-war years. A particularly bleak picture emerged from James Robb's 1947–49 study of a random sample of 103 adult males in Bethnal Green, 26 per cent of whom were judged extreme anti-Semites, just 18 per cent being tolerant of the Jews, with the other 56 per cent harbouring more latent and stereotypical attitudes against them.[103] This might be thought an exceptional case (Bethnal Green having an image before the war as one of the most strongly anti-Semitic areas in London), but Hans Eysenck's research among a more middle-class group found one-fifth of them markedly anti-Semitic.[104] The fairly poor rating of Jews was almost certainly exacerbated by the increasingly intractable question of Palestine, which had been under British mandate since 1922, and the associated post-war Jewish refugee crisis. Palestine was a responsibility that half the population wanted Britain to surrender by September 1946 (according to the *Daily Express* Poll),[105] with 57 per cent in October 1946 (Gallup) wishing the United Nations (UN) to take over the Jewish refugee crisis.[106] In February 1947 the Government did actually turn the Palestine problem over to the UN, to the endorsement of 65 per cent of voters (Gallup, March 1947),[107] and in May 1948 Britain relinquished its mandate and Israel made its unilateral declaration of independence. Public attitudes to the new Jewish state were initially (July 1948, Gallup and Research Services) ambivalent,[108] but there was a temporary thaw in 1956–57 around the Suez crisis, British support for Israel in the Middle East conflict trebling in Gallup polls between December 1955 and May 1957.[109] This doubtless impacted perceptions of Jews in Britain. Even so, as late as January 1960, one-fifth judged anti-Semitism still to be increasing.[110] Jews were deemed to have too much power by 34 per cent in August 1959,[111] with 27 per cent averse to voting for a

DOI: 10.1057/9781137512536.0009

Jewish parliamentary candidate in November 1958,[112] and 12 per cent having a poor regard for Jews in December 1961.[113] The trial of Nazi war criminal Adolf Eichmann in 1961 appears to have lifted somewhat, at least temporarily, public sympathy for both Jews and Israel (Gallup, April and August 1961).[114]

Religious attitudes to secular issues

Faith also impinged on attitudes to a range of social and ethical questions,[115] and polls investigating these did sometimes include analyses by religious affiliation. They exemplified the interaction of religion and morality, albeit it was striking how relatively few people explicitly ascribed their ethical motivations to religious origins. Invited, in three Gallup polls in December 1954,[116] February 1957,[117] and December 1963–January 1964,[118] to give reasons why they should be 'honest and truthful and kind', 'my religion tells me to' came well down the list of possible answers, alternative explanations rooted in enlightened self-interest, authoritarianism, altruism, and hedonism being much favoured. In fact, the proportion citing religious reasons unprompted was just 17 per cent in 1954, 11 per cent in 1957, and 6 per cent in 1963-64.

Breaks by religious profession for specific moral issues were not wholly consistent, but there was a tendency for Catholics to be most conservative in their views and for the religious 'nones' to be most liberal. This was even the case in a matter such as Artificial Insemination by Donor (AID), which was approved by fewer than one-quarter of all adults in Gallup polls in January 1949[119] and March 1958,[120] with a majority of Catholics (63 per cent in 1958) opposed and a plurality of 'nones' in favour; 53 per cent of Catholics in 1958 actually wanted AID to be made illegal. On this and most other morality-related topics, Protestants were positioned between these two poles of Catholics and no religionists, albeit they by no means constituted a monolithic bloc. Sundry ecumenical overtures and especially the launch of the Anglican-Methodist Conversations in 1955 led to small-scale research projects to tease out and understand the social as well as ecclesiological differences within Protestantism.[121] Temperance was an example of a legacy issue which continued to divide Protestant opinion in the long 1950s, a cause regarded as virtually synonymous with Methodism, notwithstanding the depth of Methodist commitment to it can easily be exaggerated.[122]

DOI: 10.1057/9781137512536.0009

After 1963 abortion and birth control were questions of disproportionate concern to Catholics, regularly featuring in the polls, yet they rarely did so during the preceding decade. Divorce, however, was aired in several Gallup studies, unsurprisingly given the big rise in the number of petitions for divorce filed in the post-war era. Asked in February 1952 whether they approved of all four existing grounds (desertion, cruelty, adultery, and insanity) on which a divorce could be granted, 64 per cent of all adults said they did, but the figure fell to 36 per cent of Catholics and was double that (73 per cent) for those professing no faith (with Nonconformists on 71 per cent, Anglicans on 66 per cent, and Church of Scotland adherents on 58 per cent).[123] Indeed, 49 per cent of Catholics felt in March 1958 that divorce should not be permitted under any circumstances (against just 11 per cent of the population as a whole),[124] and the proportion was still nearly one-third in July 1963.[125] A further one in six Catholics at both dates wanted divorce to be made more difficult, as did 29 per cent of Anglicans and 34 per cent of Nonconformists in 1958, with no more than one in ten desiring it to be made easier, and a plurality in all religious groups apart from Catholics in favour of the legislative *status quo*. Views were shaped by churchgoing frequency as well as by denomination, regular church attenders in December 1954 being three times more likely than non-attenders (53 versus 19 per cent) to say that it should be more difficult to divorce, with 27 per cent of non-attenders (and 6 per cent of frequent worshippers) wanting it made easier.[126] At the same time, amidst this prevailing social conservatism, there was endorsement for some specific measures of divorce liberalization. For example, two-thirds of all religious groups except Catholics in 1952 desired couples to have an automatic right to a divorce by mutual consent, even Catholics being 41 per cent in favour.[127] This represented a big shift in attitudes since March 1948, when only the religious 'nones' (45 per cent) were particularly supportive of the idea.[128] Likewise, almost three-fifths of adults voiced criticism of the Church of England's opposition to the remarriage of divorcees in April 1947,[129] November 1955,[130] and February 1957.[131]

Capital punishment was another topic which dominated public debate in the 1950s, and religion was often central to the discussion.[132] Unlike divorce, where there was arguably more of an alignment between religious opinion on the ground and the policies of the Christian Churches, the campaign to abolish the death penalty for murder (which achieved its legislative goal with temporary suspension in 1965 and permanent

DOI: 10.1057/9781137512536.0009

abolition in 1969) exemplified an issue where a generally conservative laity was at odds with a more reformist ecclesiastical leadership. The largest scale surveys on the subject during these years were conducted by M-O in April–May 1948 and December 1955–January 1956 (Table 4.5), the question being about the desirability of suspending capital punishment for a trial period of five years. It will be seen that a majority of Britons (in 1948) and a plurality (in 1955–56) disapproved of the proposal, and that, in this instance, people with no formal connection to any church were only marginally more likely than average to approve. Moreover, a plurality of Catholics was in favour of reform by 1955–56, in striking contrast to Anglicans, Nonconformists, Church of Scotland adherents, and even the religiously unaffiliated, all of whom remained ill-disposed to suspending the death penalty. Catholics were also the religious group in 1955–56 to record the lowest approval for the general principle of capital punishment, 41 per cent compared with a national average of 49 per cent and a high of 53 per cent for Anglicans.

Most of the other surveys during the long 1950s were by Gallup, whose preoccupation was to test public attitudes to the abolition, rather than the suspension, of the death penalty. Its polls in May 1947[133] and August 1949[134] revealed that, while majority opinion in all religious groups was

TABLE 4.5   *Attitudes to the suspension for five years of the death penalty for murder, Great Britain, 1948 and 1955–56 (percentages across)*

	4–5/1948 Approve	4–5/1948 Disapprove	12/1955–1/1956 Approve	12/1955–1/1956 Disapprove
All	13	69	34	45
Non-attenders	16	65	36	42
Church of England	10	72	32	48
Church of Scotland	12	70	30	44
Nonconformist	17	66	35	42
Roman Catholic	15	66	45	35
Jew	40	42	39	37
Other religion	30	50	40	37

Note: Other replies not shown. Total sample size was 6, 114 in 4–5/1948 and 6, 110 in 12/1955–1/1956.

Sources: Daily Telegraph, 28 May 1948, 13 March 1956; M-O, *Capital Punishment: A Survey Specially Conducted for the Daily Telegraph* (London: M-O, 1948), p. 12; J.B. Christoph, *Capital Punishment and British Politics: The British Movement to Abolish the Death Penalty, 1945–57* (London: George Allen and Unwin, 1962), pp. 119–20; N. Twitchell, *The Politics of the Rope: The Campaign to Abolish Capital Punishment in Britain, 1955–1969* (Bury St Edmunds: Arena, 2012), pp. 160, 166; M-OA, 1/2/72/1I, 1/2/72/3A.

DOI: 10.1057/9781137512536.0009

firmly against abolition, people of no faith took a much more liberal view than the denominationally committed. For instance, in 1947, 69 per cent of all Britons wished to see capital punishment retained with 24 per cent seeking its repeal, but among the nones the figures were, respectively, 55 and 40 per cent. The death penalty was endorsed by 74 per cent of Anglicans, 72 per cent of Scottish Presbyterians, 70 per cent of Catholics, 65 per cent of Nonconformists, and 58 per cent of those subscribing to another religion. By May–August 1963, just two years before its suspension, the British Market Research Bureau found that 81 per cent of Anglicans and 76 per cent of Catholics and other Christians continued to favour the death penalty, against 47 per cent of the nones. However, support among frequent churchgoers (73 per cent) was somewhat less than for infrequent attenders or non-attenders (both 81 per cent).[135]

Capital punishment was naturally an intensely political matter, and thus links to the relationship between religion and party political alignment. This connection was given prominence by the ground-breaking research by David Butler and Donald Stokes in 1963,[136] which foreshadowed the series of British Election Studies from 1964, trend data from which have recently been analysed by religion.[137] However, Butler and Stokes were by no means the first in the field. Several local investigations into religion and voting behaviour had been undertaken in the post-war years, including in Greenwich in 1949-50,[138] Banbury in 1950,[139] Droylsden in 1951,[140] Glossop in 1953–54,[141] Bristol North East in 1955,[142] and Newcastle-under-Lyme in 1959-60.[143] Nationally, work on religious psephology had been pursued through Gallup data collected in 1943, 1957, and 1962,[144] the immediate post-war years,[145] 1957,[146] 1963–64,[147] and 1964,[148] while there were some other academic-led investigations besides that of Butler and Stokes, such as by Robert McKenzie and Allan Silver in 1958[149] and Garry Runciman in 1962.[150] Additionally, findings from M-O's two capital punishment surveys in 1948 and 1955–56 are summarized in Table 4.6, derived from a correlation of the answers to questions on 'what Church, if any, do you usually attend?' and 'which political party, if any, do you support?'

Despite inevitable variability over time and space, some constants did emerge from these surveys, notably the greater propensity of Anglicans to support the Conservative Party and of Catholics (often the majority) to vote Labour. People of no religion also tended to favour Labour. Although only a minority of Nonconformists backed the Liberal Party (a plurality having transferred allegiance to Labour), the number who did

DOI: 10.1057/9781137512536.0009

TABLE 4.6 *Political partisanship by religion, Great Britain, 1948 and 1955–56 (percentages across)*

	4–5/1948	4–5/1948	4–5/1948	12/1955–1/1956	12/1955–1/1956	12/1955–1/1956
	Con	Lab	Lib	Con	Lab	Lib
All	40	30	6	37	35	5
Non-attenders	30	38	3	24	45	3
Church of England	52	23	4	46	30	5
Church of Scotland	40	28	5	35	35	4
Nonconformist	25	35	18	32	33	10
Roman Catholic	25	41	3	24	47	3
Jew	25	22	8	37	27	7
Other religion	27	34	8	29	32	8

Note: Other replies not shown. Total sample size was 6,114 in 4–5/1948 and 6, 110 in 12/1955–1/1956.

Sources: M-OA, 1/2/47/10E, 1/2/72/2E.

so was disproportionate to the presence of the Free Churches in society, reflecting the historical bond between Liberalism and Nonconformity. At the 1964 general election, for example, according to Gallup, Nonconformists accounted for one-tenth of the electorate but delivered 19 per cent of the Liberal vote, while in Banbury in 1950 it was as much as one-half. However, these associations need to be qualified in three ways. First, as the cohort analysis by Butler and Stokes revealed, religious cleavages in voting were not as strong as they had been in the past and were most likely to persist among the middle class. Second, the religious effect was significantly diluted once social class was controlled for; in other words, the ostensible impact of religion on voting was mainly due to the differential class basis of the respective religious groups, whose electoral behaviour was in accordance with their class pattern (the obvious example being the disproportionately working class background of Catholics). Third, the strongest links between religion and voting were rather more dependent on churchgoing (which was also impacted by class) than denomination, the greater the frequency of churchgoing, the greater the disposition to favour the Conservatives. For instance, in England as a whole in 1963-64, the two main parties stood at 33 per cent for the Conservatives and 37 per cent Labour, whereas among regular churchgoers the split was 41 and 27 per cent respectively, representing a Conservative lead of 14 per cent (and of 30 per cent in the case of Anglican churchgoers).[151]

DOI: 10.1057/9781137512536.0009

Notes

1   M-O, *Puzzled People: A Study in Popular Attitudes to Religion, Ethics, Progress, and Politics in a London Borough* (London: Victor Gollancz, 1947), pp. 7, 18–20.

2   T. Harrisson, *Britain Revisited* (London: Victor Gollancz, 1961), pp. 256–8.

3   A previous analysis is unhelpful in averaging belief data for the 1940s/1950s: R. Gill, C.K. Hadaway, and P.L. Marler, 'Is Religious Belief Declining in Britain?' *Journal for the Scientific Study of Religion*, 37 (1998), pp. 507–16.

4   For background, see W.K. Kay, 'Belief in God in Great Britain, 1945-1996: Moving the Scenery behind Classroom RE', *British Journal of Religious Education*, 20 (1997–98), pp. 28–41.

5   M-O, *Peace and the Public: A Study* (London: Longmans, Green, 1947), p. 14. Transcripts of the answers from one of these samples, in Camden Town in December 1946, are at M-OA, 1/2/47/4D.

6   M-OA, 1/2/80/2F.

7   A somewhat higher level of belief in God (84 per cent) was found by Gallup in England in December 1963–January 1964; Social Surveys (Gallup Poll), *Television and Religion* (London: University of London Press, 1964), pp. 45–7, 127.

8   Unpublished report in author's possession. National Opinion Polls still recorded belief in God at 90 per cent in April–May 1964; 'National Opinion Polls National Political Surveys', dataset at UKDA [distributor], SN 64009.

9   Unpublished material supplied by the late D.V. Glass to the author.

10 *News Chronicle*, 27 April 1939.

11 The figure was 50 per cent in England alone in December 1963–January 1964; Social Surveys (Gallup Poll), *Television and Religion*, pp. 50–1, 127.

12 G.E.S. Gorer, *Exploring English Character* (London: Cresset Press, 1955), p. 459.

13 L. Paul, *The Deployment and Payment of the Clergy: A Report* (London: Church Information Office, 1964), p. 29.

14 BBC Audience Research Department, 'Religious Broadcasts and the Public: A Social Survey of the Differences between Non-Listeners and Listeners to Religious Broadcasts' (1955), p. 37, BBC Written Archives Centre, Caversham.

15 Gorer, *Exploring English Character*, p. 458.

16 Unpublished report in author's possession.

17 *News Chronicle*, 15 April 1957; R. Stark, 'Class, Radicalism, and Religious Involvement in Great Britain', *American Sociological Review*, 29 (1964), p. 705; C.Y. Glock and R. Stark, *Religion and Society in Tension* (Chicago: Rand McNally, 1965), p. 198; Gallup, *GIPOP*, i., p. 405.

18 *Gallup Political Index*, 39 (1963), p. 75; B. Martin, 'Comments on Some Gallup Poll Statistics', in D.A. Martin, ed., *A Sociological Yearbook of Religion in Britain [1]* (London: SCM Press, 1968), pp. 155–6, 179; Gallup, *GIPOP*, i., p. 683. For

DOI: 10.1057/9781137512536.0009

England in December 1963–January 1964, see Social Surveys (Gallup Poll), *Television and Religion*, pp. 49–50, 127.

19 Gorer, *Exploring English Character*, p. 457.

20 *News Chronicle*, 15 April 1957; Stark, 'Class, Radicalism, and Religious Involvement', p. 705; Glock and Stark, *Religion and Society in Tension*, p. 198; Gallup, *GIPOP*, i., p. 405.

21 *Gallup Political Index*, 39 (1963), p. 75; Martin, 'Comments', pp. 154, 178; Gallup, *GIPOP*, i., p. 683. For England in December 1963–January 1964, see Social Surveys (Gallup Poll), *Television and Religion*, pp. 47–8, 127.

22 M-OA, 1/2/47/3D.

23 C.D. Field, '*Puzzled People* Revisited: Religious Believing and Belonging in Wartime Britain, 1939–45', *Twentieth Century British History*, 19 (2008), pp. 457–8.

24 M-O, FR 3008, 'Who Are the Astrologists?' (1948), M-OA, 1/1/13/6/4; tables at M-OA, 1/2/80/3E. M-O had previously undertaken a small-scale interview survey in London in September 1946 (see M-OA, 1/2/47/3C).

25 M-O, FR 2461A, 'Superstition' (1947), M-OA, 1/1/12/2/5, p. 1.

26 Gorer, *Exploring English Character*, pp. 477, 479, 481.

27 *News Chronicle*, 11 August 1951; Gallup, *GIPOP*, i., p. 242.

28 Gorer, *Exploring English Character*, pp. 470, 472, 474.

29 *News Chronicle*, 26 October 1949; Gallup, *GIPOP*, i., p. 208.

30 M-O, 'Do You Believe in Telepathy?' *News Review*, 30 June 1949.

31 Gallup, *GIPOP*, i., p. 405.

32 Ibid., p. 32.

33 *News Chronicle*, 12 June 1950; Gallup, *GIPOP*, i., p. 219.

34 H. Cantril, ed., *Public Opinion, 1935–1946* (Princeton: Princeton University Press, 1951), p. 836; Gallup, *GIPOP*, i., pp. 133–4; 'British Institute of Public Opinion (Gallup) Polls, 1938–1946', dataset at UKDA [distributor], SN 3331. Cf. M-O, FR 2461A, 'Superstition' (1947), M-OA, 1/1/12/2/5, based on replies from M-O's national panel.

35 K. Garwood, 'Superstition and Half Belief', *New Society*, 31 January 1963.

36 M-O, FR 2475, 'Faith and Fear in Postwar Britain' (1947), M-OA, 1/1/12/5/1, p. 21.

37 Gorer, *Exploring English Character*, pp. 464, 467.

38 Unpublished material supplied by the late D.V. Glass to the author.

39 Gallup, *GIPOP*, i., p. 677.

40 R.L. Merritt and D.J. Puchala, eds, *Western European Perspectives on International Affairs: Public Opinion Studies and Evaluations* (New York: Frederick A. Praeger, 1968), p. 199.

41 Gallup, *GIPOP*, i., p. 706.

42 *News Chronicle*, 15 April 1957; Gallup, *GIPOP*, i., p. 406.

43 Unpublished table in author's possession.

DOI: 10.1057/9781137512536.0009

44   Social Surveys (Gallup Poll), *Television and Religion*, pp. 38–9, 122.
45   Gallup, *GIPOP*, i., p. 177.
46   *News Chronicle*, 15 April 1957; Stark, 'Class, Radicalism, and Religious Involvement', pp. 704–5; Glock and Stark, *Religion and Society in Tension*, pp. 196–7; Gallup, *GIPOP*, i., p. 406.
47   For background, see C.D. Field, 'Another Window on British Secularization: Public Attitudes to Church and Clergy since the 1960s', *Contemporary British History*, 28 (2014), pp. 190–218.
48   *News Chronicle*, 3 April 1947; H.J. Eysenck, *The Psychology of Politics* (London: Routledge & Kegan Paul, 1954), p. 33; Gallup, *GIPOP*, i., p. 151.
49   *Daily Graphic*, 11 August 1948; M-OA, 1/2/47/12C.
50   *News Review*, 23 October, 6 November 1947.
51   *News Chronicle*, 15 April 1957; Gallup, *GIPOP*, i., p. 406.
52   Social Surveys (Gallup Poll), *Television and Religion*, pp. 42–4, 122–3.
53   Gallup, *GIPOP*, i., p. 458.
54   Ibid., p. 406.
55   Social Surveys (Gallup Poll), *Television and Religion*, pp. 40–2, 123.
56   *Gallup Political Index*, 37 (1963), pp. 15–16; Gallup, *GIPOP*, i., p. 667; 'Database of Selected British Gallup Opinion Polls, 1958–1991', dataset at UKDA [distributor], SN 3803 – analysis by B. Clements.
57   Harrisson, *Britain Revisited*, pp. 210–11.
58   Social Surveys (Gallup Poll), *Television and Religion*, pp. 67–72, 118, 126–7.
59   'The Five Nation Study', dataset at UKDA [distributor], SN 370.
60   Gallup, *GIPOP*, i., p. 378.
61   *News Chronicle*, 16 April 1957; Gallup, *GIPOP*, i., p. 406.
62   *Daily Express*, 8 November 1955.
63   Gallup, *GIPOP*, i., p. 406.
64   For background, see C.D. Field, '"A Quaint and Dangerous Anachronism"? Who Supports the (Dis)establishment of the Church of England?', *Implicit Religion*, 14 (2011), pp. 319–41.
65   Gallup, *GIPOP*, i., p. 256.
66   BBC Audience Research Department, 'Religious Broadcasts', pp. 27–8.
67   Gallup, *GIPOP*, i., p. 407.
68   Social Surveys (Gallup Poll), *Television and Religion*, pp. 87–9, 130.
69   *Products and People: The Reader's Digest European Surveys* (London: Reader's Digest Association, 1963), table 40.
70   Gallup, *GIPOP*, i., pp. 256–7.
71   *News Chronicle*, 12 June 1959; Gallup, *GIPOP*, i., p. 511.
72   For background, see C.D. Field, '"The Secularised Sabbath" Revisited: Opinion Polls as Sources for Sunday Observance in Contemporary Britain', *Contemporary British History*, 15 (2001), pp. 1–20; J. Wigley, *The Rise and Fall of the Victorian Sunday* (Manchester: Manchester University Press, 1980), pp. 194–5.

73   H.J.W. Legerton, *For Our Lord and His Day: A History of the Lord's Day Observance Society* (Leicester: printed by Oldham & Manton, [?1993]).

74   Home Office, *Report of the Departmental Committee on the Law on Sunday Observance* (House of Commons Papers, Session 1964–65, Cmnd. 2528, London: HMSO, 1964).

75   Ibid., p. 71; Gallup, *GIPOP*, i., pp. 466–7.

76   M-O, *Meet Yourself on Sunday* (London: Naldrett Press, 1949). Raw material for this study is at M-OA, 1/2/81.

77   A far more statistically representative source than the self-selecting samples in newspaper readership surveys at the time of lobbying against the Sunday Observance Bill 1953; *Daily Mirror*, 29 January 1953, *Daily Sketch*, 30 January 1953.

78   Home Office, *Report of the Departmental Committee*, p. 71; Gallup, *GIPOP*, i., pp. 466–7.

79   W. Hodgkins, *Sunday: Christian and Social Significance* (London: Independent Press, 1960), pp. 126–9, 226–34.

80   *Daily Mail*, 5 April 1960.

81   Gallup, *GIPOP*, i., p. 521.

82   A.J. James and J.E. Thomas, *Wales at Westminster: A History of the Parliamentary Representation of Wales, 1800–1979* (Llandysul: Gomer Press, 1981), pp. 277–8. Cf. H. Carter and J.G. Thomas, 'The Referendum on the Sunday Opening of Licensed Premises in Wales as a Criterion of a Culture Region', *Regional Studies*, 3 (1969), pp. 61–71; C.M. Wilson, 'The Sunday Opening Referenda, 1961–1989: A Study in Social and Cultural Change in Wales' (MPhil thesis, University of Wales, Aberystwyth, 1993).

83   Home Office, *Report of the Departmental Committee*, p. 71; Gallup, *GIPOP*, i., pp. 466–7.

84   *Daily Graphic*, 20 October 1948; unpublished tables at M-OA, 1/2/80/4D.

85   *Gallup Political Index*, 58 (1965), p. 12.

86   BBC Audience Research Department, 'Religious Broadcasts', pp. 18–19.

87   Social Surveys (Gallup Poll), *Television and Religion*, pp. 52–7, 125–6.

88   *News Chronicle*, 15 April 1957; Gallup, *GIPOP*, i., p. 405.

89   Social Surveys (Gallup Poll), *Television and Religion*, pp. 38, 122.

90   Gallup, *GIPOP*, i., pp. 321, 327.

91   M-O, FR 2387, 'Report on Attitudes to the Salvation Army' (1946), M-OA, 1/1/11/4/4. Raw material for this study is at M-OA, 1/2/47/8.

92   *News Chronicle*, 6 February 1959; *The Scotsman*, 6 February 1959; R. Glass, *Newcomers: The West Indians in London* (London: Centre for Urban Studies, 1960), pp. 248–50; Gallup, *GIPOP*, i., p. 545.

93   Social Surveys (Gallup Poll), *Television and Religion*, pp. 35, 121.

94   For background, see C.D. Field, 'No Popery's Ghost: Does Popular Anti-Catholicism Survive in Contemporary Britain?', *Journal of Religion in Europe*,

7 (2014), pp. 116–49. There is no full-scale history of anti-Catholicism in twentieth-century Britain as a whole, although there are useful insights in J.R. Wolffe, 'Change and Continuity in British Anti-Catholicism, 1829-1982', in F. Tallett and N. Atkin, eds, *Catholicism in Britain and France since 1789* (London: Hambledon Press, 1996), pp. 67–83.

95   For background, see C.D. Field, 'John Bull's Judeophobia: Images of the Jews in British Public Opinion Polls since the Late 1930s', *Jahrbuch für Antisemitismusforschung*, 15 (2006), pp. 259–300. In addition to polling evidence, Field also cites some of the mixed methods research by M-O at this time, which features in T. Kushner, *We Europeans? Mass-Observation, 'Race', and British Identity in the Twentieth Century* (Aldershot: Ashgate, 2004). Raw material survives in M-OA for M-O's sub-national surveys, of attitudes to Jews in 1946 (M-OA, 1/2/62/3A) and 1950 (1/2/62/4B-D), and to the Palestine question in 1946 (1/2/62/3B) and 1947 (1/2/62/3C-E).

96   S.H. Mayor, 'The Religion of the British People', *Hibbert Journal*, 49 (1960-61), p. 40.

97   Gallup, *GIPOP*, i., p. 523.

98   Ibid., p. 405.

99   *Gallup Political Index*, 25 (1962), p. 19; Gallup, *GIPOP*, i., p. 617.

100   *News Chronicle*, 6 February 1959; *The Scotsman*, 6 February 1959; Glass, *Newcomers*, pp. 248–50; Gallup, *GIPOP*, i., p. 545.

101   *Gallup Political Index*, 23 (1961), p. 45, 42 (1963), p. 129; Gallup, *GIPOP*, i., pp. 607, 688–9, 697.

102   Social Surveys (Gallup Poll), *Television and Religion*, pp. 60–2, 123.

103   J.H. Robb, *Working-Class Anti-Semite: A Psychological Study in a London Borough* (London: Tavistock Publications, 1954), p. 92.

104   H.J. Eysenck, 'Primary Social Attitudes, I. The Organization and Measurement of Social Attitudes', *International Journal of Opinion and Attitude Research*, 1 (1947), pp. 49–84; idem, 'The Psychology of Anti-Semitism', *The Nineteenth Century and After*, 144 (1948), pp. 277–84; H.J. Eysenck and S. Crown, 'An Experimental Study in Opinion-Attitude Methodology', *International Journal of Opinion and Attitude Research*, 3 (1949), pp. 47–86.

105   *Daily Express*, 9 September 1946.

106   *News Chronicle*, 14 November 1946; Cantril, *Public Opinion*, p. 387; Gallup, *GIPOP*, i., p. 140.

107   Gallup, *GIPOP*, i., p. 153.

108   Ibid., i., p. 179; M.A. Abrams, 'British Opinion and the Recognition of Israel', *Public Opinion Quarterly*, 13 (1949), pp. 128–30.

109   Merritt and Puchala, *Western European Perspectives on International Affairs*, pp. 431–4.

110   Gallup, *GIPOP*, i., p. 489.

111   Ibid., p. 523.
112   *News Chronicle*, 6 February 1959; *The Scotsman*, 6 February 1959; Glass, *Newcomers*, pp. 248–50; Gallup, *GIPOP*, i., p. 545.
113   *Gallup Political Index*, 25 (1962), p. 19; Gallup, *GIPOP*, i., p. 617.
114   *Gallup Political Index*, 17 (1961), pp. 19–20, 21 (1961), p. 25; Gallup, *GIPOP*, i., pp. 583, 595.
115   For background, see G.I.T. Machin, 'British Churches and Social Issues, 1945–60', *Twentieth Century British History*, 7 (1996), pp. 345–70; idem, *Churches and Social Issues in Twentieth-Century Britain* (Oxford: Clarendon Press, 1998), pp. 137–74.
116   BBC Audience Research Department, 'Religious Broadcasts', pp. 29–33.
117   Gallup, *GIPOP*, i., p. 405.
118   Social Surveys (Gallup Poll), *Television and Religion*, pp. 73–6, 119.
119   *News Chronicle*, 21 February 1949.
120   Unpublished table in author's possession.
121   Perhaps the best-known example of such an investigation in the Anglican-Methodist context was D.B. Clark, *Survey of Anglicans and Methodists in Four Towns* (London: Epworth Press, 1965), based on research in 1962–64.
122   C.D. Field, ' "The Devil in Solution": How Temperate Were the Methodists?', *Epworth Review*, 27 (2000), pp. 78–93. Temperance sentiments among the Nonconformist ministry were surveyed by the Christian Economic and Social Research Foundation: *Methodist Ministers and Total Abstinence: Report on an Enquiry Made with the Goodwill of the Christian Citizenship Department of the Methodist Church* (London: the Foundation, 1962) and *Ministers of the Congregational Church and Presbyterian Church of England and Total Abstinence* (London: the Foundation, 1962).
123   Unpublished report in author's possession.
124   Unpublished table in author's possession.
125   *Sunday Telegraph*, 4 August 1963.
126   BBC Audience Research Department, 'Religious Broadcasts', p. 38.
127   Unpublished report in author's possession.
128   *News Chronicle*, 15 April 1948.
129   Gallup, *GIPOP*, i., p. 157.
130   Ibid., pp. 359–60.
131   *News Chronicle*, 16 April 1957; Gallup, *GIPOP*, i., p. 406.
132   For background, see H. Potter, *Hanging in Judgment: Religion and the Death Penalty in England from the Bloody Code to Abolition* (London: SCM Press, 1993), pp. 142–203; H. McLeod, 'God and the Gallows: Christianity and Capital Punishment in the Nineteenth and Twentieth Centuries', in K. Cooper and J. Gregory, eds, *Retribution, Repentance, and Reconciliation* (*Studies in Church History*, 40, Woodbridge: Boydell Press, 2004), pp. 330–56; and N. Twitchell, *The Politics of the Rope: The Campaign to Abolish*

DOI: 10.1057/9781137512536.0009

Capital Punishment in Britain, 1955–1969 (Bury St Edmunds: Arena, 2012), pp. 128–55.

133 J.B. Christoph, *Capital Punishment and British Politics: The British Movement to Abolish the Death Penalty, 1945–57* (London: George Allen and Unwin, 1962), p. 44; Twitchell, *Politics of the Rope*, p. 157.

134 *News Chronicle*, 10 October 1949.

135 'Political Change in Britain, 1963–1970', dataset at UKDA [distributor], SN 44 – analysis by B. Clements.

136 D.H.E. Butler and D.E. Stokes, *Political Change in Britain: The Evolution of Electoral Choice* (2nd edn, London: Macmillan, 1974), pp. 156–65. Their data were reworked by W.L. Miller and G. Raab, 'The Religious Alignment at English Elections between 1918 and 1970', *Political Studies*, 25 (1977), pp. 227–51.

137 B. Clements and N. Spencer, *Voting and Values in Britain: Does Religion Count?* (London: Theos, 2014), pp. 29–35.

138 M. Benney, A.P. Gray, and R.H. Pear, *How People Vote: A Study of Electoral Behaviour in Greenwich* (London: Routledge & Kegan Paul, 1956), p. 111.

139 M. Stacey, *Tradition and Change: A Study of Banbury* (London: Oxford University Press, 1960), pp. 39–40.

140 P. Campbell, D. Donnison, and A. Potter, 'Voting Behaviour in Droylsden in October 1951', *Manchester School of Economic and Social Studies*, 20 (1952), p. 63.

141 A.H. Birch, *Small-Town Politics: A Study of Political Life in Glossop* (London: Oxford University Press, 1959), pp. 88, 112.

142 R.S. Milne and H.C. Mackenzie, *Marginal Seat, 1955: A Study of Voting Behaviour in the Constituency of Bristol North East at the General Election of 1955* (London: Hansard Society for Parliamentary Government, 1958), pp. 65–6, 70–1.

143 F. Bealey, J. Blondel, and W.P. McCann, *Constituency Politics: A Study of Newcastle-Under-Lyme* (London: Faber and Faber, 1965), p. 173.

144 R.R. Alford, *Party and Society: The Anglo-American Democracies* (London: John Murray, 1964), pp. 105, 134–41.

145 Eysenck, *Psychology*, p. 21.

146 Stark, 'Class, Radicalism, and Religious Involvement', pp. 698–706; Glock and Stark, *Religion and Society in Tension*, pp. 193–9.

147 Social Surveys (Gallup Poll), *Television and Religion*, pp. 16–18.

148 *The Gallup Election Handbook, March 1966* (London: Social Surveys, Gallup Poll, 1966), p. B8; R. Rose, 'Party Systems, Social Structure, and Voter Alignments in Britain: A Guide to Comparative Analysis', in O. Stammer, ed., *Party Systems, Party Organizations, and the Politics of New Masses* (Berlin: Institut für Politische Wissenschaft an der Freien Universität Berlin, 1968),

DOI: 10.1057/9781137512536.0009

pp. 318–84; 'Gallup General Election Surveys, 1964', dataset at UKDA [distributor], SN 2051.

149   R. McKenzie and A. Silver, *Angels in Marble: Working Class Conservatives in Urban England* (London: Heinemann Educational, 1968), pp. 100–1; 'Angels in Marble: Working Class Conservatives in Urban England, 1958–1960', dataset at UKDA [distributor], SN 7429.

150   W.G. Runciman, *Relative Deprivation and Social Justice: A Study of Attitudes to Social Inequality in Twentieth-Century England* (London: Routledge & Kegan Paul, 1966), pp. 174–5.

151   Social Surveys (Gallup Poll), *Television and Religion*, pp. 16–17.

DOI: 10.1057/9781137512536.0009

5
Conclusion

Abstract: *The conclusion reprises, in turn, the findings of Chapters 2, 3, and 4, concerning, respectively, religious belonging, religious behaviour, and religious beliefs. The chapter thus provides a holistic picture, as defined by statistics, of the religious landscape of 1950s' Britain. In turn, this enables a summative evaluation of Brown's claims for the religious nature of the 1950s and its increasingly gendered basis. In essence, these claims are rejected on quantitative grounds and reasons given for doing so. It is contended that the 1950s are perhaps still best understood in the context of a progressive and protracted secularization of the role of religion in British life. This leaves Brown's case primarily dependent upon qualitative evidence and arguments for the cultural significance of Christianity.*

Keywords: 1950s; Callum Brown; religious behaviour; religious beliefs; religious belonging; secularization

Field, Clive D. *Britain's Last Religious Revival? Quantifying Belonging, Behaving, and Believing in the Long 1950s.* Basingstoke: Palgrave Macmillan, 2015. DOI: 10.1057/9781137512536.0010.

DOI: 10.1057/9781137512536.0010

Belonging

In terms of self-identification, Britain remained a religious (and over-whelmingly Christian) society during the long 1950s. Sample survey data (Table 2.1) suggest that religious affiliation among adults was high and fairly stable throughout the entire period. The number professing no religion was less than 10 per cent and no more than 6 per cent in the poll, in 1963, with the largest sample. This figure was only marginally up on the 4 per cent for 'nones' estimated on the eve of the Second World War (Table 2.2). According to subsequent Gallup and National Opinion Polls,[1] this remained the case throughout the 1960s and 1970s, also, notwithstanding the so-called religious crisis of the 1960s. The majority of the population (61 per cent in Table 2.2) aligned with the Church of England, whose market share actually appears to have increased since *c*. 1939, at the expense of the Free and Presbyterian Churches, which collectively lost ground (from 29 per cent in *c*. 1939 to 22 per cent in *c*. 1963). There was little change between these two dates in the propor-tion of adults professing to be Roman Catholics or non-Christians. In very many (perhaps most) cases, according to the retrospective polling, these denominational allegiances were not always strongly held, nor were strenuous efforts made by many parents to pass them on to their children. One traditional pillar of religious socialization – via the family – was therefore crumbling, helping pave the way for secularization.

The pattern for church membership is harder to describe, owing to the multiplicity of criteria for defining membership. Nevertheless, a broad distinction can be drawn between religious groups, notably Catholic, Orthodox, Jew, and other non-Christian, whose membership was defined as coterminous with the total constituency of the group (including chil-dren), and the Protestant Churches, which mostly restricted member-ship to adults and those in late adolescence. In both instances numbers obviously need to be examined relative to the growth in population, and not just absolutely (between 1945 and 1963 the mid-year population of Britain is estimated to have risen by 9 per cent or 8 per cent for adults alone). Even on the imperfect *Catholic Directory* statistics (Table 2.6), the increase in the Catholic community from 1945 to 1963 was impressive, 48 per cent in Britain, 56 per cent in England and Wales, and 22 per cent in Scotland. If we use instead the sacramental index favoured by the NDS ('four-wheeler' Catholics who participated in all the Church's rites of passage), there were 6,373,000 Catholics in Britain in 1963

DOI: 10.1057/9781137512536.0010

(12 per cent of the population and 17 per cent in Scotland), although by this time leakage was beginning to emerge as a serious problem. Catholic growth was driven by mixed marriages, above average fertility, conversions, and – most of all – by immigration, not least from Ireland. Immigration also explains the 161 per cent expansion in the number of Orthodox Christians during the long 1950s and the more than doubling of non-Christians other than Jews, to reach 100,000 by the early 1960s. Jews, by contrast, contracted by 9 per cent over the period. Immigrant communities typically had a disproportionately youthful profile, which partly helps explain why their growth was not necessarily fully reflected in surveys of religious profession among adults.

Within Protestantism, the Anglicans generally fared better than non-Anglicans in terms of membership, although the picture in the Church of England very much depended upon the performance measure examined. Electoral roll membership fell continuously, both absolutely and relatively. Confirmations were largely stable as a proportion of baptisms 13 years before but demonstrated a slight improvement (until 1960) when expressed as a ratio of the English population aged 12–20 or of names on the electoral roll. The most flattering index of all was that of Easter communicants, up by 25 per cent between 1947 and 1962, with a peak in 1956 at 7 per cent of the adult population, followed by a levelling out. Communicant numbers also rose strongly in the Church in Wales, albeit not in the Episcopal Church of Scotland. However, the encouragement to the Church of England provided by these communicant data should not be allowed to disguise the low membership baseline from which it was operating, which materially explains why, in terms of the three home nations, church membership as a proportion of the population was by far the lowest in England, still considerably exceeded by Wales (thanks to the historic predominance of Nonconformity) and even more so by Scotland (where Presbyterianism was preponderant). According to John Highet (Table 2.5), almost three-fifths of Scottish adults were church members in these years, two-thirds of them being Presbyterians. Allowing for data missing from Highet's 1947 calculation, these proportions did not vary greatly.

According to Table 2.7, actual and estimated membership of all the Free Church and Presbyterian denominations reduced by 3 per cent from 1945 to 1963, or from just under 10 per cent of adults to just under 9 per cent. The historic Free Churches suffered most, and nowhere more so than in Wales, where the Calvinistic Methodists contracted by

DOI: 10.1057/9781137512536.0010

26 per cent. In Britain Congregational decline was relentless, year on year, with the number of Congregational members in England falling below the Baptist total for the first time. It would have been a similarly depressing story for the Baptists and Methodists in Britain, were it not for extremely modest and temporary recoveries in 1954–56 and 1948–54, respectively. The Church of Scotland's overall advance to 1963 was a mere 1 per cent, although its communicants grew by 5 per cent from 1947 to 1956 and active communicants by 9 per cent from 1948 to 1955. Other success stories, from modest starting-points, were registered by Pentecostalists (underpinned by immigration from the West Indies), Jehovah's Witnesses, and Latter-Day Saints. The membership of the various bodies committed to organized irreligion was tiny and, in aggregate, stable at around 10,000.

Decline in Free Church membership was exacerbated by further erosion in the number of non-member adherents (down by one-third from *c.* 1939) and continuing recession in Sunday school numbers, both potential sources of recruits for new members. Whereas nine-tenths of all adults had been to Sunday school when they were growing up, only just over half their own children were attending in the 1940s and 1950s. Even the short-term increase in scholars between 1948 and 1953 (except in the Presbyterian Church of Wales) failed to keep pace with the growth in the population aged 3–17. By 1963 the combined Sunday scholars of the five principal English and Welsh Free Churches were 33 per cent less than they had been in 1945 and 39 per cent less than in 1953. The Church of Scotland was again something of an exception, growth in its Sunday scholars being sustained until 1956 and also being especially large (32 per cent since 1945).

Behaving

Callum Brown's case for 'revolutionary secularization' in the 1960s, and for an associated 'religious boom' during the 1950s, is potentially contradicted by Britain's increasingly well-documented churchgoing history. It is significant that, in one of his most recent writings, Brown makes a preemptive strike by simultaneously criticizing the exponents of gradualist secularization for an over-dependence on church attendance evidence and by attempting to put a positive gloss on the British data available for the 1950s. However, he concedes that Britain 'had a markedly lower

DOI: 10.1057/9781137512536.0010

level of church attendance by the 1950s' than other western nations, and that 'this started some time before'.[2] In fact, the single most authoritative overview of the topic, by Robin Gill,[3] argues that, relative to population, attendances in the Church of England and Congregationalism had been declining from the 1850s and in the Free Churches generally since the 1880s. The progressive nature of churchgoing decline is also suggested by studies of shorter periods in the twentieth century. For example, in partial qualification of Brown's claim that the Edwardian era was 'the faith society', it has been shown that average national weekly attendance had already reduced to one-quarter of adults, disproportionately women, with some two-fifths worshipping at least monthly.[4] During the inter-war years decline accelerated, the historic Free Churches being most seriously impacted; there was also decreased regularity of worship (linked to the diversification of secular leisure destinations and easier access to them) and the first sign of the ageing of Protestant congregations.[5]

In the aggregate, churchgoing appears to have diminished still further during the long 1950s, but perhaps not at any rapid pace, certainly until the late 1950s. The exception was Catholic Mass attendance which rose in line with Catholic population growth. Three separate measures point to an average weekly participation rate by about one person in seven in Great Britain, which was less than before the Second World War. Estimates from church-based sources for *c.* 1960 produce a figure of 14 per cent. Local surveys (Table 3.1) clustered in the 10–15 per cent range, highs being associated with a strong Catholic presence (which explains the 20 per cent achieved in Glasgow in 1954). The most robust opinion poll data, asking Britons about church attendance on the Sunday prior to interview, reveal a decline from 15 per cent in 1948 to 12 per cent in 1958.

All three measures exhibit the demographic variations displayed in earlier periods. In sub-national terms, weekly churchgoing was lowest in England (13 per cent on the church-based estimates for *c.* 1960), higher in Wales (22 per cent), and highest of all in Scotland (26 per cent), although the Scottish figure represented less than half of those in church membership in 1959. Attendance tended to be better in the countryside than towns, and it was worst of all in the major cities, notably London. Women were far more likely to worship on a weekly basis than men, older generations than family-formers and the middle-aged, and those in non-manual occupations more than manual ones. Denominationally, Catholics were most dutiful (as many as 41 per cent attending on an ordinary Sunday in England and Wales in the early 1960s and 53 per cent

DOI: 10.1057/9781137512536.0010

in Scotland), and professing Anglicans the least. Table 5.1 illustrates the likely attrition of non-communicating Anglican regular churchgoers during the twentieth century.

Attendance at church on an average Sunday naturally does not tell the full story since many worshipped on a less regular basis. The polls (Table 3.2) suggest that non-attenders never exceeded one-half of adults, sometimes considerably fewer, and that between one-quarter and one-third claimed to worship at least once a month, which would be the accepted definition of regular churchgoing today. As previously noted, due allowance needs to be made for the potential, indeed probable, exaggeration of all such claims. The attraction of special services in the ecclesiastical calendar (such as Easter, Christmas, Harvest Festival, and Armistice Sunday) explains some of this pattern of irregularity, but much seems to have become routinized. Whereas people had formerly

TABLE 5.1   *Conjectural religious profile of adult population, Great Britain, c. 1914, c. 1939, and c. 1963 (percentages down)*

	1914	1939	1963	1963
	%	%	%	Persons
Anglicans				
Communicants	9	7	7	2,585,000
Other regular churchgoers	15	8	2	1,000,000
Occasional churchgoers/nominal affiliates	40	40	52	20,425,000
Sub-total	64	55	61	24,010,000
Roman Catholics				
Baptised persons known to priests	6	6	8	3,310,000
Nominal affiliates	NA	5	2	630,000
Sub-total	NA	11	10	3,940,000
Free Churches/Presbyterians				
Members	13	10	9	3,430,000
Adherents	11	4	2	1,000,000
Nominal affiliates	4	16	11	4,150,000
Sub-total	28	30	22	8,580,000
Others				
Non-Christians	1	1	1	470,000
No religion	1	4	6	2,360,000

Note: In working from community figures, and deducting children, allowance has been made for the fact that Roman Catholics and Jews had above-average family sizes.

Sources: Religion data for *c.* 1914 from C.D. Field, ' "The Faith Society"? Quantifying Religious Belonging in Edwardian Britain, 1901–1914', *Journal of Religious History*, 37 (2013), p. 62; for *c.* 1939 from C.D. Field, 'Gradualist or Revolutionary Secularization? A Case Study of Religious Belonging in Inter-War Britain, 1918–1939', *Church History and Religious Culture*, 93 (2013), p. 91; and for *c.* 1963 extracted and extrapolated from the text of this book.

DOI: 10.1057/9781137512536.0010

attended church twice on a Sunday, they now attended only once, while weekly attendance was increasingly exchanged for every other week or every few weeks. In some cases broadcast religious services and programmes, on radio and television, were allowed to become a 'substitute' for frequenting public worship, although their combined audiences were contracting. Mostly, however, people were finding other things to do, inside and outside the home, on a Sunday, with television a definite counter-attraction to evening churchgoing by the end of the long 1950s. Greater car ownership (from 14 per cent of households in 1951 to 29 per cent in 1960) may also have increased the temptation to reduce churchgoing.[6] Sunday was thus well on the way to its transformation into 'the weekend'.[7]

The reach of the Churches was at its most extensive in terms of the occasional offices which celebrated significant moments in personal and family lives – the rites of passage. The ecclesiastical monopoly of such events was especially secure in respect of funerals, hardly any of which were conducted without religious ceremony. Baptism also commanded near-universal support, in excess of nine-tenths of babies being christened, but the allied rite of churching (a service of purification, blessing, and thanksgiving for the new mother) was in decline, dying out rapidly from the late 1960s. Marriage in a place of worship was more pervasive than churching, if not quite as ubiquitous as funerals and baptisms. Statistics for both England and Wales and Scotland are only available for four years during the long 1950s (1952, 1957, and 1962–63), with a combined mean of 71 per cent of weddings solemnized in churches (70 per cent in England and Wales and 81 per cent in Scotland). There was some fluctuation in the annual series for Scotland alone, with a high of 86 per cent in 1945 and a low of 80 per cent in 1962–63. The greater disposition to religious marriage in Scotland doubtless reflected the much higher incidence of church membership there than in England and Wales. The majority of all these rites of passage were conducted by the Church of England in England and the Church of Scotland in Scotland. Their (for the most part) continuing popularity may have had as much to do with social custom and expectation as religious devotion. The services were probably not often understood in what the Churches would have considered to be theologically orthodox terms and attendance at, and the demand for, them was essentially a component of folk religion, as Sarah Williams discovered for the pre-war years.[8]

DOI: 10.1057/9781137512536.0010

Information about private religious practices is very limited and only available through opinion polls, which are likely to be subject to some inflation. Although Bibles could be found in around nine-tenths of households, they were rarely consulted, especially by men and the young, regular reading being claimed by just 12 per cent of all adults in England in 1963–64. Just under one-half claimed to pray on their own regularly, more so among women and the elderly, far fewer than felt it desirable for children to be taught to say their prayers.

Believing

The long 1950s was the first period when, through opinion polls, popular beliefs could be quantitatively and representatively investigated at national level. Prior to that time, only qualitative exploration was generally possible, through local studies which have often been enriched by oral testimony. Several modern qualitative accounts have demonstrated that popular religion – beyond the Churches – was, in reality, a rich tapestry woven from an odd blend of orthodoxy, heterodoxy, superstition, and folklore.[9] Or, as a contemporary Congregational minister put it: 'the religion of the British people is not recognizably traditional Christianity, but neither is it a rival system of belief. It is a curious mixture of orthodox doctrines, variegated heresies, and naïve speculations.'[10] M-O, through its classic study of *Puzzled People*, based on wartime research in Hammersmith in 1944–45, entered this hybrid intellectual world, but its coverage was far from exhaustive, and its 1960 replication is apparently lost. We are, therefore, necessarily dependent upon the more piecemeal questioning that found its way on to omnibus surveys of the general British public.

Of the various orthodox measures, belief in God was held by about four-fifths of adults, with just over half this number believing in a personal God and the remainder in a spirit or vital force. According to Gallup, belief in God declined somewhat throughout the 1950s. Belief in Jesus was likewise around four-fifths, albeit a diminishing number was convinced of His divinity. Belief in life after death was maintained by far fewer, approximately half the population, although many struggled to define what form it would take, beyond rejecting the notion of hell. Heterodox beliefs were subscribed to by a minority in the late 1940s, ranging from 10 per cent in the case of ghosts

DOI: 10.1057/9781137512536.0010

to 39 per cent for telepathy. However, practice was often at odds with stated conviction, many taking refuge in ambivalent or uncertain answers. Thus, whereas only 22 per cent said they believed in astrology in 1947, 71 per cent admitted to consulting horoscopes in newspapers and magazines regularly or occasionally in 1951. Likewise, more people had visited a fortune-teller than claimed to believe in foretelling the future. Regrettably, there are no published cross-correlations showing what overlap existed between orthodox and heterodox beliefs, although it is clear that women disproportionately believed in both. Orthodox beliefs tended to increase with age, but it could work the other way for heterodox beliefs. For example, in 1946 those in their twenties were 10 points more superstitious than average and almost as superstitious as women.

The effects of these beliefs, whether orthodox or heterodox, on every-day behaviour and attitudes were generally not documented, but some evidence does exist for the outworking of religious identity and attend-ance. However, we should be mindful of the potential risks of assuming causation from correlation and also aware of the seeming contradictions which surfaced in the replies to pollsters' questions. As a broad generali-zation, Britons of the 1950s did not take up a uniformly traditional and conservative position when it came to religious issues in the public square. This was not a monolithically 'puritan' society, as might be inferred from Brown's work. Indeed, only just over one-quarter in 1963 actually thought of themselves as religious, and still fewer cited religion as the source of authority for their personal morality. The majority felt that religion's hold over national life was diminishing, and a plurality backed the separation of Church and State. There was substantial generic criticism of Churches and clergy and, in presumed deference to Protestantism, lingering mani-festations of prejudice against specific religious groups, notably Catholics and Jews. There was growing public support for the campaign to liberal-ize the law on Sunday observance, with 47 per cent in 1958 wanting to see Sunday treated no differently, in legislative terms, than any other day of the week. Modernization of the Sunday statutes was particularly desired in respect of licensed premises, places of entertainment, and sport. There was even significant endorsement for reform of the divorce laws, while three-fifths expressed displeasure at the Church of England's opposi-tion to the remarriage of divorcees. This is not to deny the existence of a strong caucus of social conservatism, but it was disproportionately located among churchgoers and Catholics. A counter-culture was clearly

DOI: 10.1057/9781137512536.0010

emerging in the 1950s which sought to challenge a traditional religious worldview. Symptomatic of this transition was the weakening influence of religious cleavages on electoral behaviour.

Summative assessment

Callum Brown has suggested that the 1950s in Britain witnessed 'something of a religious boom', exemplified in 'one of the most concerted periods of church growth since the middle of the nineteenth century'. The decade was characterized by a 'return to piety', and 'people's lives ... were very acutely affected by genuflection to religious symbols, authority and activities'. These claims are supported in his published work by a range of evidence, much of it of a qualitative nature, especially autobiography and oral history, in respect of 'discursive Christianity'. However, he also utilizes quite a lot of statistics. In this book, we have drawn upon the widest available range of quantitative data (emanating from the Churches, opinion poll and other social research organizations, and individual academics) to test Brown's arguments in the light of three contrasting dimensions of religiosity – belonging, behaving, and believing. Having travelled this course, we must now conclude that, whatever the grounds for thinking there was 'a renaissance in British Christian culture', Brown's case for church growth is overstated.

That Britain remained, in certain respects, a religious (essentially Christian) nation cannot be denied. More than nine persons in ten identified with a denomination, four-fifths believed in God and Jesus Christ, and the Bible was to be found in nine-tenths of homes. But there is nothing to suggest that these proportions were any higher in the 1950s than they had been in preceding decades, and they were, in any case, very passive and nominal indicators of religiosity. There were certainly decided limits to the lengths to which parents went to transmit their religion to their children, apart from pinning faith in religious education in state schools and in a Sunday school movement which, overall, continued to contract, notwithstanding opportunities presented by spurts in the birth rate. As retrospective polling, through pooled British Social Attitudes Surveys, has demonstrated, religious decline in twentieth-century Britain has been overwhelmingly generational, with each birth cohort less religious than the one before.[11] This diminution in religious socialization is already evident in the 1950s.

DOI: 10.1057/9781137512536.0010

Churching apart, which was decreasingly observed, the rites of passage likewise continued to be accompanied by religious ceremonies (virtually 100 per cent in the case of funerals, at least 90 per cent of baptisms, and 70 per cent of marriages). However, for many families, their religious significance was subservient to the social and any supernatural dimension was as likely to be rooted in folklore as in orthodox Christianity. Moreover, far from there being any greater 'genuflection' to religious authority in the 1950s, the polls suggest that some elements of the public were beginning to criticize Churches and clergy and to seek liberalization of statutory restrictions strongly associated with organized religion. Although many of those restrictions were ultimately only eased or abolished from the 1960s onwards, the ground was already being prepared by attitudinal shifts in the 1950s.

As for church growth, it is hard to identify any of a substantive kind which was not driven by demographic changes, and particularly by immigration. Roman Catholicism was the success story of the decade, from this perspective, but it does not appear to be central to Brown's thesis. On a basket of metrics of belonging and behaving, the 1950s appear to have been a decade of decline for most of the historic Free Churches, while growth in the Church of England and the Church of Scotland was limited in scale and time and, crucially, it mostly did not keep pace with population increase (except for Sunday scholars in the Kirk). Growth which is only absolute and not relative is, some might contend, no growth at all. Additionally, in the Anglican case, growth never extended to the electoral rolls (the formal criterion of membership) and such as occurred elsewhere was from a very low baseline. The Church of Scotland's starting-point was much higher, yet its concept of membership was apparently quite diluted (demonstrated by the fact that nearly one-third of its communicants were officially recorded as inactive and weekly churchgoing in the Scottish Churches was less than half the membership).

Similarly, there may have been (as Brown suggests) 'immense popularity for evangelical "revivalist" crusades', in the sense that large numbers attended (in particular) the Billy Graham missions of 1954–55. Yet, discounting for multiple visits to the events, the overwhelming majority of the nation did not directly hear his message. Graham may have given a boost to the evangelical movement in general and help revitalize the Evangelical Alliance in particular,[12] but he appears to have made no real numerical difference to the religious landscape, other than a slight and

DOI: 10.1057/9781137512536.0010

very temporary improvement in the membership recruitment rates of the Baptist Church and the Church of Scotland and in Protestant church attendance in Glasgow. For the most part, Graham was preaching to those within the church family, and, in so far as he 'converted' outsiders, only a minority persisted in their religious journeys.

In general, churchgoing continued on its longstanding downward path, especially in terms of weekly attendance, with severe losses of non-communicant regular Anglican worshippers and adherents in the Free and Presbyterian Churches (Table 5.1). To an extent, television and car ownership competed with the Churches for people's time on Sundays. Church attendance continued to be skewed in terms of sex, age, region, and social class. But Brown's notion that religious adherence and practice became more gendered in the 1950s is firmly substantiated through statistics only by a minimal increase in female confirmands in the Church of England, while it is undermined by the progressive demise of the churching of women after childbirth. In all other respects, the greater religiosity of women over men seems to have been much as it had been for decades (arguably for centuries) previously.[13]

The weakness in Brown's argument is similar to one which has bedevilled a recent upbeat assessment of church growth in Britain since the 1980s, to which Steve Bruce has rightly objected.[14] The existence of spatial and/or temporal pockets of growth is accepted, but they do not transform the overall picture. Ever since the Methodists pioneered the collection of religious statistics in the 1760s, church growth and decline have co-existed. What matters is the net direction of travel (once the arithmetical subtractions have been done) compared with movements in the population. From this standpoint, the 1950s were not some pinnacle of religious revivalism. With only the rarest of exceptions,[15] contemporary ecclesiastical observers did not view them in that light (on the contrary, the prevailing mood was one of pessimism), and they were surely right not to. At the start of the long 1950s, M-O estimated that 10–15 per cent of the population was closely linked to a Christian church, with a further 25–30 per cent sufficiently interested to attend worship occasionally, 45–50 per cent indifferent to religion albeit more or less friendly disposed to it, and 10–20 per cent as positively hostile.[16] Towards the end of the decade, *The Economist* concluded that, notwithstanding lower levels of anti-clericalism than in many other countries, 'less than a quarter take their religious observances seriously' and that 'about 70 per cent of

DOI: 10.1057/9781137512536.0010

people regard the Christian religion as a good thing provided it does not interfere with their private lives'.[17]

So, despite the odd flicker of hope, the 1950s are perhaps still best understood in the context of a progressive and protracted secularization of the role of religion in British life, a process which had already started before that decade and which continued long afterwards. The actual pace of decline was uneven – from one denomination to another, from one part of the country to another, and from one indicator of religiosity to another – but the trajectory is unmistakeable. The findings of the present research, from a different and broader evidence base, therefore accord with several of Brown's peers who have already concluded that his religious assessment of the 1950s should be, in large part, rejected. This is not to deny, nor is it contradicted by, the existence of a deep vein of 'discursive Christianity' in the land, which many commentators feel survived the 1950s and 1960s and even continues to this day, albeit transmuted and reinvented.[18] The strength of feeling on this subject was revealed in the public and media debate in the spring and early summer of 2014, to which the Prime Minister contributed, about whether Britain was or should be a Christian country.[19]

It has not been our purpose here to examine the claims made by Brown and other scholars for revolutionary secularization occurring in 1960s' Britain (although we have noted that the 'religious crisis' did not lead to any precipitate and large-scale increase in those professing no faith). But the quantitative source material to scrutinize these claims is even more extensive than for the 1950s, so perhaps that will be our next task. Meanwhile, we must thank Brown and other historians and sociologists for their stimulating contributions to the literature of British secularization and hope that, through ongoing debate and the presentation of new evidence, the chronology and nature of religious change in modern Britain can be further clarified and illuminated.

Notes

1   C.D. Field, 'Measuring Religious Affiliation in Great Britain: The 2011 Census in Historical and Methodological Context', *Religion*, 44 (2014), pp. 371–2.

2   C.G. Brown, *Religion and the Demographic Revolution: Women and Secularisation in Canada, Ireland, UK, and USA since the 1960s* (Woodbridge: Boydell Press, 2012), pp. 39, 43, 72–89.

DOI: 10.1057/9781137512536.0010

3 R. Gill, *The 'Empty' Church Revisited* (Aldershot: Ashgate, 2003).

4 C.D. Field, '"The Faith Society"? Quantifying Religious Belonging in Edwardian Britain, 1901–1914', *Journal of Religious History*, 37 (2013), pp. 41–53, 61.

5 C.D. Field, 'Gradualist or Revolutionary Secularization? A Case Study of Religious Belonging in Inter-War Britain, 1918–1939', *Church History and Religious Culture*, 93 (2013), pp. 62–78, 90.

6 R.P.M. Sykes, 'Popular Religion in Dudley and the Gornals, c. 1914–1965' (PhD thesis, University of Wolverhampton, 1999), pp. 334–7.

7 W.S.F. Pickering, 'The Secularized Sabbath: Formerly Sunday, Now the Weekend', in M. Hill, ed., *A Sociological Yearbook of Religion in Britain*, 5 (London: SCM Press, 1972), pp. 33–47.

8 S.C. Williams, 'Urban Popular Religion and the Rites of Passage', in H. McLeod, ed., *European Religion in the Age of Great Cities, 1830–1930* (London: Routledge, 1995), pp. 216–36.

9 For example, D. Clark, *Between Pulpit and Pew: Folk Religion in a North Yorkshire Fishing Village* (Cambridge: Cambridge University Press, 1982); S.C. Williams, *Religious Belief and Popular Culture in Southwark, c. 1880–1939* (Oxford: Oxford University Press, 1999); Sykes, 'Popular Religion in Dudley and the Gornals'.

10 S.H. Mayor, 'The Religion of the British People', *Hibbert Journal*, 49 (1960–61), p. 38.

11 A. Crockett and D. Voas, 'Generations of Decline: Religious Change in 20th-Century Britain', *Journal for the Scientific Study of Religion*, 45 (2006), pp. 567–84.

12 I.M. Randall and D. Hilborn, *One Body in Christ: The History and Significance of the Evangelical Alliance* (Carlisle: Paternoster Press, 2001), pp. 216–30.

13 For a broader discussion of this phenomenon, see M. Trzebiatowska and S. Bruce, *Why Are Women More Religious than Men?* (Oxford: Oxford University Press, 2012).

14 D. Goodhew, ed., *Church Growth in Britain, 1980 to the Present* (Farnham: Ashgate, 2012) and the ensuing debate in *Journal of Religion in Europe*, 6 (2013): S. Bruce, 'Secularization and Church Growth in the United Kingdom', pp. 273–96, D. Goodhew, 'Church Growth in Britain', pp. 297–315, S. Bruce, 'Further Thoughts on Church Growth and Secularization', pp. 316–20.

15 For example, M. Argyle, *Religious Behaviour* (London: Routledge & Kegan Paul, 1958), pp. 25, 27, who found 'some evidence of a general revival in British churches since 1950'.

16 M-O, FR 2475, 'Faith and Fear in Postwar Britain' (1947), M-OA, 1/1/12/5/1, pp. 9–10.

17 Anon, 'How Many in the Pew?', *The Economist*, 30 August 1958.

DOI: 10.1057/9781137512536.0010

18   See, especially, J. Garnett, M. Grimley, A. Harris, W. Whyte, and S.C.
      Williams, eds, *Redefining Christian Britain: Post-1945 Perspectives* (London:
      SCM Press, 2006).

19   For trend opinion poll data on this subject from 1965 onwards, see C.D.
      Field, 'Christian Country and Other News', *British Religion in Numbers*, 27
      April 2014, http://www.brin.ac.uk/news/2014/christian-country-and-other-
      news/.

DOI: 10.1057/9781137512536.0010

Bibliography

This bibliography records substantive printed primary and secondary sources referenced in the endnotes, omitting brief news reports cited only by serial title and date. It is sub-divided between contemporary and later works, the former published between 1945 and 1963 or, if slightly later, based on research completed by 1963; the latter published after 1963, including some volumes which are effectively primary sources in providing digests of religious statistics for the 1950s. Other printed sources consulted during the preparation of this book but not cited therein are excluded.

Contemporary Works

Abrams, M.A., 'British Opinion and the Recognition of Israel', *Public Opinion Quarterly*, 13 (1949), pp. 128–30.

——, *Social Surveys and Social Action* (London: William Heinemann, 1951).

——, *The Teenage Consumer* (London: London Press Exchange, 1959).

Alan, P., 'The Statistics of Belief', *The Humanist*, 76 (1961), pp. 169–71.

Alford, R.R., *Party and Society: The Anglo-American Democracies* (London: John Murray, 1964).

Allan, T., ed., *Crusade in Scotland: Billy Graham* (London: Pickering & Inglis, 1955).

Anon, 'How Many in the Pew?' *The Economist*, 30 August 1958.

DOI: 10.1057/9781137512536.0011

Argyle, M., *Religious Behaviour* (London: Routledge & Kegan Paul, 1958).

Banks, J.A., 'The Sociology of Religion in England', *Sociologische Gids*, 10 (1963), pp. 45–50.

Bealey, F., Blondel, J., and McCann, W.P., *Constituency Politics: A Study of Newcastle-under-Lyme* (London: Faber and Faber, 1965).

Beck, G.A., 'To-Day and To-Morrow', in G.A. Beck, ed., *The English Catholics, 1850–1950: Essays to Commemorate the Centenary of the Restoration of the Hierarchy of England and Wales* (London: Burns Oates, 1950), pp. 585–614.

Benney, M., Gray, A.P., and Pear, R.H., *How People Vote: A Study of Electoral Behaviour in Greenwich* (London: Routledge & Kegan Paul, 1956).

Birch, A.H., *Small-Town Politics: A Study of Political Life in Glossop* (London: Oxford University Press, 1959).

Birnbaum, N., 'La sociologie de la religion en Grande-Bretagne', *Archives de Sociologie des Religions*, 1 (1956), pp. 3–16.

——, 'Soziologie der Kirchengemeinde in Grossbritannien', in D. Goldschmidt, F. Greiner, and H. Schelsky, eds, *Soziologie der Kirchengemeinde* (Stuttgart: Ferdinand Enke, 1960), pp. 49–65.

Bliss, K., 'Opinion Polls', *Christian News-Letter*, 24 November 1948.

Bracey, H.E., *English Rural Life* (London: Routledge & Kegan Paul, 1959).

Brothers, J.B., 'Recent Developments in the Sociology of Religion in England and Wales', *Social Compass*, 11 (1964), pp. 13–19.

——, 'Religion in the British Universities: The Findings of Some Recent Surveys', *Archives de Sociologie des Religions*, 9 (1964), pp. 71–82.

Budd, S., 'The Humanist Societies: The Consequences of a Diffuse Belief System', in B.R. Wilson, ed., *Patterns of Sectarianism: Organisation and Ideology in Social and Religious Movements* (London: Heinemann, 1967), pp. 366–405.

Busia, K.A., *Urban Churches in Britain: A Question of Relevance* (London: Lutterworth Press, 1966).

Butler, D.E. and Freeman, J., *British Political Facts, 1900–1960* (London: Macmillan, 1963).

Butler, J.R., 'A Sociological Study of Lapsed Membership', *London Quarterly and Holborn Review*, 191 (1966), pp. 236–44.

Callard, P., 'The Church and Older People', *Social Service Quarterly*, 33 (1959-60), pp. 115–18.

Calley, M.J.C., *God's People: West Indian Pentecostal Sects in England* (London: Oxford University Press, 1965).

DOI: 10.1057/9781137512536.0011

Campbell, C.B., 'Membership Composition of the British Humanist Association', *Sociological Review*, 13 (1965), pp. 327–37.

Campbell, P., Donnison, D., and Potter, A., 'Voting Behaviour in Droylsden in October 1951', *Manchester School of Economic and Social Studies*, 20 (1952), pp. 57–65.

Cantril, H., ed., *Public Opinion, 1935–1946* (Princeton: Princeton University Press, 1951).

Carr-Saunders, A.M., Jones, D.C., and Moser, C.A., *A Survey of Social Conditions in England and Wales as Illustrated by Statistics* (Oxford: Clarendon Press, 1958).

Carter, H. and Thomas, J.G., 'The Referendum on the Sunday Opening of Licensed Premises in Wales as a Criterion of a Culture Region', *Regional Studies*, 3 (1969), pp. 61–71.

Cassam, I., 'An Analysis of Church Affiliations in Wales', *Western Mail and South Wales News*, 30 January 1953.

——, 'Survey of Welsh Religious Life', *Western Mail and South Wales News*, 10–12 January 1952.

Cauter, T. and Downham, J., *The Communication of Ideas: A Study of Contemporary Influences on Urban Life* (London: Chatto & Windus, 1954).

Chesser, E., *The Sexual, Marital, and Family Relationships of the English Woman* (London: Hutchinson's Medical Publications, 1956).

Chou, R.-C. and Brown, S., 'A Comparison of the Size of Families of Roman Catholics and Non-Catholics in Great Britain', *Population Studies*, 22 (1968), pp. 51–60.

Christian Economic and Social Research Foundation, *Aspects of the Problem Facing the Churches* (London: the Foundation, 1960).

——, *Methodist Ministers and Total Abstinence: Report on an Enquiry Made with the Goodwill of the Christian Citizenship Department of the Methodist Church* (London: the Foundation, 1962).

——, *Ministers of the Congregational Church and Presbyterian Church of England and Total Abstinence* (London: the Foundation, 1962).

——, *Setting Up a Home* (London: the Foundation, 1957).

Christoph, J.B., *Capital Punishment and British Politics: The British Movement to Abolish the Death Penalty, 1945–57* (London: George Allen and Unwin, 1962).

Churchill, R.C., *The English Sunday* (London: Watts, 1954).

Clark, D.B., *Survey of Anglicans and Methodists in Four Towns* (London: Epworth Press, 1965).

DOI: 10.1057/9781137512536.0011

Colquhoun, F., *Harringay Story: The Official Record of the Billy Graham Greater London Crusade, 1954* (London: Hodder and Stoughton, 1955).

Commission on Evangelism of the Church Assembly, *Towards the Conversion of England* (London: Press and Publications Board of the Church Assembly, 1945).

Council for Wales and Monmouthshire, *Report on the Welsh Language Today* (House of Commons Papers, Session 1963–64, Cmnd. 2198, London: HMSO, 1963).

Davison, R.B., *Black British: Immigrants to England* (London: Oxford University Press, 1966).

Dinwiddie, M., *Religion by Radio: Its Place in British Broadcasting* (London: George Allen & Unwin, 1968).

Dodd, P., 'Who Goes to Church?', *New Society*, 29 April 1965.

Doig, D.H., *The Membership of the Church of England: Changes in Recent Years* (London: Church Information Office, 1960).

Durant, H. and Gregory, W., *Behind the Gallup Poll, with a Detailed Analysis of the 1951 General Election* ([London]: News Chronicle, [1951]).

Emmett, I., *A North Wales Village: A Social Anthropological Study* (London: Routledge & Kegan Paul, 1964).

Eysenck, H.J., 'Primary Social Attitudes, I. The Organization and Measurement of Social Attitudes', *International Journal of Opinion and Attitude Research*, 1 (1947), pp. 49–84.

——, 'The Psychology of Anti-Semitism', *The Nineteenth Century and After*, 144 (1948), pp. 277–84.

——, *The Psychology of Politics* (London: Routledge & Kegan Paul, 1954).

Eysenck, H.J. and Crown, S., 'An Experimental Study in Opinion-Attitude Methodology', *International Journal of Opinion and Attitude Research*, 3 (1949), pp. 47–86.

Frankenberg, R., *Village on the Border: A Social Study of Religion, Politics, and Football in a North Wales Community* (London: Cohen & West, 1957).

Free Church Federal Council, *Sunday Schools Today: An Investigation of Some Aspects of Christian Education in English Free Churches* (London: Free Church Federal Council, [1956]).

Garbett, C.F., *The Church of England To-Day* (London: Hodder and Stoughton, 1953).

Garwood, K., 'Superstition and Half Belief', *New Society*, 31 January 1963.

DOI: 10.1057/9781137512536.0011

Glass, R., *Newcomers: The West Indians in London* (London: Centre for Urban Studies, 1960).

Glock, C.Y. and Stark, R., *Religion and Society in Tension* (Chicago: Rand McNally, 1965).

Gorer, G.E.S., *Death, Grief, and Mourning in Contemporary Britain* (London: Cresset Press, 1965).

——, *Exploring English Character* (London: Cresset Press, 1955).

Gould, J. and Esh, S., eds, *Jewish Life in Modern Britain* (London: Routledge and Kegan Paul, 1964).

Grubb, K.G., ed., *World Christian Handbook* (London: World Dominion Press, 1949, 1952, 1957, 1962).

Harris, C.C., 'Church, Chapels, and the Welsh', *New Society*, 21 February 1963.

Harrisson, T., *Britain Revisited* (London: Victor Gollancz, 1961).

Havighurst, R.J., 'Life beyond Family and Work', in E.W. Burgess, ed., *Aging in Western Societies* (Chicago: University of Chicago Press, 1960), pp. 299–353.

Herron, S., 'What's Left of Harringay?' *British Weekly*, 10 February 1955.

Highet, J., 'The Churches', in A.K. Cairncross, ed., *The Scottish Economy: A Statistical Account of Scottish Life* (Cambridge: Cambridge University Press, 1954), pp. 297–315.

——, 'The Churches', in J. Cunnison and J.B.S. Gilfillan, eds, *The Third Statistical Account of Scotland: Glasgow* (Glasgow: Collins, 1958), pp. 713–50.

——, 'The Churches in Glasgow', *British Weekly*, 22 August 1957.

——, *The Churches in Scotland To-Day: A Survey of Their Principles, Strength, Work, and Statements* (Glasgow: Jackson, 1950).

——, 'Churchgoing in Scotland', *New Society*, 26 December 1963.

——, 'Faithful after a Fashion', *Glasgow Herald*, 11 October 1965.

——, 'Great Britain: Scotland', in H. Mol., ed., *Western Religion: A Country by Country Sociological Inquiry* (The Hague: Mouton, 1972), pp. 249–69.

——, 'How Religious is Scotland?', *Glasgow Herald*, 5 January 1968.

——, 'The Protestant Churches in Scotland: A Review of Membership, Evangelistic Activities, and Other Aspects', *Archives de Sociologie des Religions*, 4 (1959), pp. 97–104.

——, 'A Review of Scottish Socio-Religious Literature', *Social Compass*, 11 (1964), pp. 21–4.

DOI: 10.1057/9781137512536.0011

——, *The Scottish Churches: A Review of Their State 400 Years after the Reformation* (London: Skeffington, 1960).

——, 'Scottish Religious Adherence', *British Journal of Sociology*, 4 (1953), pp. 142–59.

——, 'Trend Report on the Sociology of Religion in Scotland', *Social Compass*, 13 (1966), pp. 343–8.

Hill, C., *West Indian Migrants and the London Churches* (London: Oxford University Press, 1963).

Hodgkins, W., *Sunday: Christian and Social Significance* (London: Independent Press, 1960).

Holt, I.L. and Clark, E.T., *The World Methodist Movement* (Nashville: The Upper Room, 1956).

Home Office, *Report of the Departmental Committee on the Law on Sunday Observance* (House of Commons Papers, Session 1964-65, Cmnd. 2528, London: HMSO, 1964).

Hyde, K.E., *Religious Learning in Adolescence* (Edinburgh: Oliver and Boyd, 1965).

Independent Television Authority, *Religious Programmes on Independent Television* (London: Independent Television Authority, 1962).

Jackson, J.A., *The Irish in Britain* (London: Routledge & Kegan Paul, 1963).

Jennings, H., *Societies in the Making: A Study of Development and Redevelopment within a County Borough* (London: Routledge & Kegan Paul, 1962).

Kaim-Caudle, P.R., 'Church & Social Change: A Study of Religion in Billingham, 1959–66', *New Christian*, 9 March 1967.

——, *Religion in Billingham, 1957–59* (Billingham-on-Tees: Billingham Community Association, 1962).

Layton, G., 'Religion', *The Navy*, 52 (1947), pp. 147–8.

Lewis-Faning, E., *Report on an Enquiry into Family Limitation and its Influence on Human Fertility during the Past Fifty Years* (Papers of the Royal Commission on Population, 1, London: HMSO, 1949).

Macleod, R.D., 'Church Statistics for England', *Hibbert Journal*, 46 (1948), pp. 351–7.

Macmillan, F., 'The Faithful of Scotland: A Statistical Enquiry', *The Tablet*, 25 July 1959.

Martin, B., 'Comments on Some Gallup Poll Statistics', in D.A. Martin, ed., *A Sociological Yearbook of Religion in Britain [1]* (London: SCM Press, 1968), pp. 146–97.

DOI: 10.1057/9781137512536.0011

Martin, D.A., 'Interpreting the Figures', in M. Perry, ed., *Crisis for Confirmation* (London: SCM Press, 1967), pp. 106–15.

——, *A Sociology of English Religion* (London: SCM Press, 1967).

Mass-Observation, *Capital Punishment: A Survey Specially Conducted for the Daily Telegraph* (London: Mass-Observation, 1948).

——, *Contemporary Churchgoing* (London: Mass-Observation, 1949).

——, 'Do You Believe in Telepathy?' *News Review*, 30 June 1949.

——, *Meet Yourself on Sunday* (London: Naldrett Press, 1949).

——, *Peace and the Public: A Study* (London: Longmans, Green, 1947).

——, *Puzzled People: A Study in Popular Attitudes to Religion, Ethics, Progress, and Politics in a London Borough* (London: Victor Gollancz, 1947).

Mayor, S.H., 'The Religion of the British People', *Hibbert Journal*, 49 (1960-61), pp. 38–43.

Mays, J.B., 'New Hope in Newtown', *New Society*, 22 August 1963.

McKenzie, R. and Silver, A., *Angels in Marble: Working Class Conservatives in Urban England* (London: Heinemann Educational, 1968).

McNarney, M., 'La vie paroissiale', in *Catholicisme anglais* (Paris: Éditions du Cerf, 1958), pp. 146–70.

McNicol, J., ed., *Free Church Directory, 1965–66* (Morden: Crown House Publications, 1965).

Methodist Church, *Rural Methodism: Commission's Report to 1958 Conference* (London: Epworth Press, 1958).

Milne, R.S. and Mackenzie, H.C., *Marginal Seat, 1955: A Study of Voting Behaviour in the Constituency of Bristol North East at the General Election of 1955* (London: Hansard Society for Parliamentary Government, 1958).

Mogey, J.M., *Family and Neighbourhood: Two Studies in Oxford* (London: Oxford University Press, 1956).

Moore-Darling, E., 'Why Villagers Do Not Go to Church', *The Countryman*, 33 (1946), pp. 52–4.

Neuss, R.F., *Facts and Figures about the Church of England, Number 3* (London: Church Information Office, 1965).

Neustatter, H., 'Demographic and Other Statistical Aspects of Anglo-Jewry', in M. Freedman, ed., *A Minority in Britain: Social Studies of the Anglo-Jewish Community* (London: Vallentine, Mitchell, 1955), pp. 53–133, 243–62.

Owen, T.M., 'Chapel and Community in Glan-llyn, Merioneth', in E. Davies and A.D. Rees, eds, *Welsh Rural Communities* (Cardiff: University of Wales Press, 1960), pp. 185–248.

DOI: 10.1057/9781137512536.0011

Pahl, R.E., 'Newcomers in Town and Country', in L.M. Munby, ed., *East Anglian Studies* (Cambridge: W. Heffer & Sons, 1968), pp. 174–99.

Patterson, S.C., *Dark Strangers: A Sociological Study of the Absorption of a Recent West Indian Migrant Group in Brixton, South London* (London: Tavistock Publications, 1963).

Paul, L., *The Deployment and Payment of the Clergy: A Report* (London: Church Information Office, 1964).

Pickering, W.S.F., 'The Place of Religion in the Social Structure of Two English Industrial Towns (Rawmarsh, Yorkshire and Scunthorpe, Lincolnshire)' (PhD thesis, University of London, 1958).

——, 'The Present Position of the Anglican and Methodist Churches in the Light of Available Statistics', in W.S.F. Pickering, ed., *Anglican-Methodist Relations: Some Institutional Factors* (London: Darton, Longman & Todd, 1961), pp. 1–36.

——, 'Quelques résultats d'interviews religieuses', in Conférence Internationale de Sociologie Religieuse, *Vocation de la sociologie religieuse: sociologie des vocations* (Tournai: Casterman, 1958), pp. 54–76.

——, ' "Religious Movements" of Church Members in Two Working-Class Towns in England', *Archives de Sociologie des Religions*, 11 (1961), pp. 129–40.

Pons, V.G., 'The Social Structure of a Hertfordshire Parish' (PhD thesis, University of London, 1955).

Prais, S.J. and Schmool, M., 'The Size and Structure of the Anglo-Jewish Population, 1960–65', *Jewish Journal of Sociology*, 10 (1968), pp. 5–34.

Reader's Digest, *Products and People: The Reader's Digest European Surveys* (London: Reader's Digest Association, 1963).

——, *The Reader's Digest Complete Atlas of the British Isles* (London: Reader's Digest Association, 1965).

Reed, B.H., *Eighty Thousand Adolescents: A Study of Young People in the City of Birmingham* (London: Allen & Unwin, 1950).

Rees, A.D., *Life in a Welsh Countryside: A Social Study of Llanfihangel yng Ngwynfa* (Cardiff: University of Wales Press, 1950).

Rich, D., 'Spare Time in the Black Country', in L. Kuper, ed., *Living in Towns* (London: Cresset Press, 1953), pp. 295–370.

Richardson, I.M., *Age and Need: A Study of Older People in North-East Scotland* (Edinburgh: E. & S. Livingstone, 1964).

Robb, J.H., *Working-Class Anti-Semite: A Psychological Study in a London Borough* (London: Tavistock Publications, 1954).

DOI: 10.1057/9781137512536.0011

Roberts, C.A., ed., *These Christian Commando Campaigns: An Interpretation* (London: Epworth Press, 1945).

Roberts, W.N.T., 'Why Do Catholics Lapse? I. The Size of the Problem', *The Tablet*, 9 May 1964.

Rose, R., 'Party Systems, Social Structure, and Voter Alignments in Britain: A Guide to Comparative Analysis', in O. Stammer, ed., *Party Systems, Party Organizations, and the Politics of New Masses* (Berlin: Institut für Politische Wissenschaft an der Freien Universität Berlin, 1968), pp. 318–84.

Rosser, C. and Harris, C.C., *The Family and Social Change: A Study of Family and Kinship in a South Wales Town* (London: Routledge & Kegan Paul, 1965).

Rowntree, B.S. and Lavers, G.R., *English Life and Leisure: A Social Study* (London: Longmans, Green, 1951).

Runciman, W.G., *Relative Deprivation and Social Justice: A Study of Attitudes to Social Inequality in Twentieth-Century England* (London: Routledge & Kegan Paul, 1966).

Sampson, A., *Anatomy of Britain* (London: Hodder and Stoughton, 1962).

Sandhurst, B.G. [pseudonym of C.H. Green], *How Heathen is Britain?* (London: Collins, 1946, rev. edn, 1948).

Schofield, M.G., *The Sexual Behaviour of Young People* (London: Longmans, 1965).

Shannon, W., 'A Geography of Organised Religion in Liverpool' (BA dissertation, University of Liverpool, 1965).

Shenfield, B.E., *Social Policies for Old Age: A Review of Social Provision for Old Age in Great Britain* (London: Routledge and Kegan Paul, 1957).

Silvey, R.J.E., 'The Audiences for Religious Broadcasts', in *Religion on the Air: Three Talks Given to the St Paul's Lecture Society* (London: British Broadcasting Corporation, 1956), pp. 5–14.

Social Surveys (Gallup Poll), *The Gallup Election Handbook, March 1966* (London: Social Surveys, Gallup Poll, 1966).

——, *Survey of Readership of Newspapers, England and Wales* (London: Gallup Poll, 1952).

——, *Television and Religion* (London: University of London Press, 1964).

Spencer, A.E.C.W. (ed. M.E. Daly), *Arrangements for the Integration of Irish Immigrants in England and Wales* (Dublin: Irish Manuscripts Commission, 2012).

DOI: 10.1057/9781137512536.0011

——, 'The Demography and Sociography of the Roman Catholic Community of England and Wales', in L. Bright and S. Clements, eds, *The Committed Church* (London: Darton, Longman & Todd, 1966), pp. 60–85.

——, 'An Evaluation of Roman Catholic Educational Policy in England and Wales, 1900–1960', in P. Jebb, ed., *Religious Education: Drift or Decision?* (London: Darton, Longman & Todd, 1968), pp. 165–221.

——, 'The Newman Demographic Survey, 1953–62: Nine Years of Progress', *Wiseman Review*, 236 (1962), pp. 139–54.

——, 'The Newman Demographic Survey, 1953–1964: Reflection on the Birth, Life, and Death of a Catholic Institute for Socio-Religious Research', *Social Compass*, 11 (1964), pp. 31–40.

——, 'Numbering the People: Should the Census Ask About Religion?', *The Tablet*, 22 April 1961.

——, *Report on the Parish Register, Religious Practice & Population Statistics of the Catholic Church in Scotland, 1967* (Harrow: Pastoral Research Centre, 1969).

——, *The Selection of a Date for the Annual Count of Mass Attendance: A Report* (Taunton: Russell-Spencer, 2005).

——, 'Youth and Religion', *New Life*, 14 (1958), pp. 1–59.

Spinks, G.S., *Religion in Britain since 1900* (London: Andrew Dakers, 1952).

Stacey, M., *Tradition and Change: A Study of Banbury* (London: Oxford University Press, 1960).

Stark, R., 'Class, Radicalism, and Religious Involvement in Great Britain', *American Sociological Review*, 29 (1964), pp. 698–706.

Sutherland, J., *Godly Upbringing: A Survey of Sunday Schools and Bible Classes in the Church of Scotland* (Edinburgh: Church of Scotland Youth Committee, 1960).

Townsend, P. and Tunstall, S., 'Isolation, Desolation, and Loneliness', in E. Shanas, P. Townsend, D. Wedderburn, H. Friis, P. Milhøj, and J. Stehouwer, *Old People in Three Industrial Societies* (London: Routledge and Kegan Paul, 1968), pp. 258–87.

University of Sheffield Institute of Education, *Religious Education in Secondary Schools: A Survey and a Syllabus* (London: Thomas Nelson, 1961).

Varney, P.D., 'Religion in Rural Norfolk', in D.A. Martin and M. Hill, eds, *A Sociological Yearbook of Religion in Britain*, 3 (London: SCM Press, 1970), pp. 65–77.

DOI: 10.1057/9781137512536.0011

Ward, C.K., 'Sociological Research in the Sphere of Religion in Great Britain', *Sociologia Religiosa*, 3 (1959), pp. 79–94.

Wickham, E.R., *Church and People in an Industrial City* (London: Lutterworth Press, 1957).

Williams, W.M., *The Sociology of an English Village: Gosforth* (London: Routledge & Kegan Paul, 1956).

——, *A West Country Village, Ashworthy: Family, Kinship, and Land* (London: Routledge & Kegan Paul, 1963).

Willmott, P., *The Evolution of a Community: A Study of Dagenham after Forty Years* (London: Routledge & Kegan Paul, 1963).

Willmott, P. and Young, M., *Family and Class in a London Suburb* (London: Routledge & Kegan Paul, 1960).

Wilson, B.R., *Religion in Secular Society: A Sociological Comment* (London: C.A. Watts, 1966).

Wollen, D., 'Sociology and the Church Membership Committee', *London Quarterly and Holborn Review*, 188 (1963), pp. 26–33.

Wright, D., *Attitudes towards the Church in Wellingborough* (Leicester: Department of Adult Education, Leicester University, 1965).

Young, M. and Willmott, P., *Family and Kinship in East London* (London: Routledge & Kegan Paul, 1957).

Zbyszewski, W.A., 'The Catholics of England and Wales: The Reasons for Thinking They May Be Ten Per Cent of the Population', *The Tablet*, 6 March 1948.

Later Works

Ansari, H., *'The Infidel Within': Muslims in Britain since 1800* (London: Hurst, 2004).

Argent, A., *The Transformation of Congregationalism, 1900–2000* (Nottingham: Congregational Federation, 2013).

Bardgett, F.D., 'The Tell Scotland Movement: Failure and Success', *Records of the Scottish Church History Society*, 38 (2008), pp. 105–50.

Barnes, T., *Songs of Praise: Celebrating 50 Years* (Oxford: Lion, 2011).

Brewitt-Taylor, S., 'The Invention of a "Secular Society"? Christianity and the Sudden Appearance of Secularization Discourses in the British National Media, 1961–4', *Twentieth Century British History*, 24 (2013), pp. 327–50.

DOI: 10.1057/9781137512536.0011

Brierley, P.W., *A Century of British Christianity: Historical Statistics, 1900–1985* (Bromley: MARC Europe, 1989).

——, 'Religion', in A.H. Halsey and J. Webb, eds, *Twentieth-Century British Social Trends* (Basingstoke: Macmillan, 2000), pp. 650–74.

——, *Religion in Britain, 1900 to 2000* (London: Christian Research, 1998).

——, ed., *UK Christian Handbook, Religious Trends, No. 2, 2000/01 Millennium Edition* (London: Christian Research, 1999).

——, ed., *UK Christian Handbook, Religious Trends, No. 3, 2002/2003* (London: Christian Research, 2001).

——, ed., *UK Church Statistics, 2005–2015* (Tonbridge: ADBC Publications, 2011).

Briggs, A., *The History of Broadcasting in the United Kingdom, Volume IV: Sound and Vision* (Oxford: Oxford University Press, 1979).

Brothers, J.B., *Religious Institutions* (London: Longman, 1971).

Brown, C.G., *The Death of Christian Britain: Understanding Secularisation, 1800–2000* (2nd edn, London: Routledge, 2009).

——, 'Gender, Christianity, and the Rise of No Religion: The Heritage of the Sixties in Britain', in N. Christie and M. Gauvreau, eds, *The Sixties and Beyond: Dechristianization in North America and Western Europe, 1945–2000* (Toronto: University of Toronto Press, 2013), pp. 39–59.

——, 'Gendering Secularisation: Locating Women in the Transformation of British Christianity in the 1960s', in I. Katznelson and G. Stedman Jones, eds, *Religion and the Political Imagination* (Cambridge: Cambridge University Press, 2010), pp. 275–94.

——, 'Masculinity and Secularisation in Twentieth-Century Britain', in Y.M. Werner, ed., *Christian Masculinity: Men and Religion in Northern Europe in the 19th and 20th Centuries* (Leuven: Leuven University Press, 2011), pp. 47–59.

——, *The People in the Pews: Religion and Society in Scotland since 1780* (Glasgow: Economic and Social History Society of Scotland, 1993).

——, 'Religion and Secularisation', in T. Dickson and J.H. Treble, eds, *People and Society in Scotland, III, 1914–1990* (Edinburgh: John Donald, 1992), pp. 48–79.

——, *Religion and Society in Scotland since 1707* (Edinburgh: Edinburgh University Press, 1997).

——, *Religion and Society in Twentieth-Century Britain* (Harlow: Pearson, 2006).

DOI: 10.1057/9781137512536.0011

——, *Religion and the Demographic Revolution: Women and Secularisation in Canada, Ireland, UK, and USA since the 1960s* (Woodbridge: Boydell Press, 2012).

——, 'A Revisionist Approach to Religious Change', in S. Bruce, ed., *Religion and Modernization: Sociologists and Historians Debate the Secularization Thesis* (Oxford: Clarendon Press, 1992), pp. 31–58.

——, 'The Secularisation Decade: What the 1960s Have Done to the Study of Religious History', in H. McLeod and W. Ustorf, eds, *The Decline of Christendom in Western Europe, 1750–2000* (Cambridge: Cambridge University Press, 2003), pp. 29–46.

——, 'Sex, Religion, and the Single Woman, *c.* 1950–75: The Importance of a "Short" Sexual Revolution to the English Religious Crisis of the Sixties', *Twentieth Century British History*, 22 (2011), pp. 189–215.

——, 'Unfettering Religion: Women and the Family Chain in the Late Twentieth Century', in J. Doran, C. Methuen, and A. Walsham, eds, *Religion and the Household* (*Studies in Church History*, 50, Woodbridge: Boydell Press, 2014), pp. 469–91.

——, '"The Unholy Mrs Knight" and the BBC: Secular Humanism and the Threat to the "Christian Nation", *c.* 1945–60', *English Historical Review*, 127 (2012), pp. 345–76.

——, 'What Was the Religious Crisis of the 1960s?', *Journal of Religious History*, 34 (2010), pp. 468–79.

——, 'Women and Religion in Britain: The Autobiographical View of the Fifties and Sixties', in C.G. Brown and M. Snape, eds, *Secularisation in the Christian World: Essays in Honour of Hugh McLeod* (Farnham: Ashgate, 2010), pp. 159–73.

Brown, C.G. and Lynch, G., 'Cultural Perspectives', in L. Woodhead and R. Catto, eds, *Religion and Change in Modern Britain* (London: Routledge, 2012), pp. 329–51.

Bruce, S., 'Further Thoughts on Church Growth and Secularization', *Journal of Religion in Europe*, 6 (2013), pp. 316–20.

——, 'Religion in Ashworthy, 1958–2011: A Sociology Classic Revisited', *Rural Theology*, 11 (2013), pp. 92–102.

——, 'Religion in Gosforth, 1951–2011: A Sociology Classic Revisited', *Rural Theology*, 11 (2013), pp. 39–49.

——, 'Religion in Rural Wales: Four Restudies', *Contemporary Wales*, 23 (2010), pp. 219–39.

DOI: 10.1057/9781137512536.0011

——, 'Secularization and Church Growth in the United Kingdom', *Journal of Religion in Europe*, 6 (2013), pp. 273–96.

——, *Secularization: In Defence of an Unfashionable Theory* (Oxford: Oxford University Press, 2011).

——, 'A Sociology Classic Revisited: Religion in Banbury', *Sociological Review*, 59 (2011), pp. 201–22.

Bruce, S. and Glendinning, T., 'When Was Secularization? Dating the Decline of the British Churches and Locating Its Cause', *British Journal of Sociology*, 61 (2010), pp. 107–26.

Budd, S., *Varieties of Unbelief: Atheists and Agnostics in English Society, 1850–1960* (London: Heinemann, 1977).

Butler, D.H.E. and Stokes, D.E., *Political Change in Britain: The Evolution of Electoral Choice* (2nd edn, London: Macmillan, 1974).

Campbell, C.B., 'Humanism in Britain: The Formation of a Secular Value-Oriented Movement', in D.A. Martin, ed., *A Sociological Yearbook of Religion in Britain,* 2 (London: SCM Press, 1969), pp. 157–72.

——, *Toward a Sociology of Irreligion* (London: Macmillan, 1971).

Chadwick, O., *The Christian Church in the Cold War* (London: Allen Lane, 1992).

Christopher, A.J., 'The Religious Question in the United Kingdom Census, 1801–2011', *Journal of Ecclesiastical History*, 65 (2014), pp. 601–19.

Clark, D., *Between Pulpit and Pew: Folk Religion in a North Yorkshire Fishing Village* (Cambridge: Cambridge University Press, 1982).

Clements, B. and Spencer, N., *Voting and Values in Britain: Does Religion Count?* (London: Theos, 2014).

Crockett, A. and Voas, D., 'Generations of Decline: Religious Change in 20th-Century Britain', *Journal for the Scientific Study of Religion*, 45 (2006), pp. 567–84.

Currie, R., Gilbert, A.D., and Horsley, L., *Churches and Churchgoers: Patterns of Church Growth in the British Isles since 1700* (Oxford: Clarendon Press, 1977).

Darragh, J., 'The Catholic Population of Scotland, 1878–1977', in D. McRoberts, ed., *Modern Scottish Catholicism, 1878–1978* (Glasgow: Burns, 1979), pp. 211–47.

Delaney, E., *The Irish in Post-War Britain* (Oxford: Oxford University Press, 2007).

Field, C.D., 'Adam and Eve: Gender in the English Free Church Constituency', *Journal of Ecclesiastical History*, 44 (1993), pp. 63–79.

DOI: 10.1057/9781137512536.0011

——, 'Another Window on British Secularization: Public Attitudes to Church and Clergy since the 1960s', *Contemporary British History*, 28 (2014), pp. 190–218.

——, 'Demography and the Decline of British Methodism: I. Nuptiality', *Proceedings of the Wesley Historical Society*, 58 (2012), pp. 175–89.

——, 'Demography and the Decline of British Methodism: II. Fertility', *Proceedings of the Wesley Historical Society*, 58 (2012), pp. 200–15.

——, 'Demography and the Decline of British Methodism, III: Mortality', *Proceedings of the Wesley Historical Society*, 58 (2012), pp. 247–63.

——, ' "The Devil in Solution": How Temperate Were the Methodists?', *Epworth Review*, 27 (2000), pp. 78–93.

——, 'Faith in the Metropolis: Opinion Polls and Christianity in Post-War London', *London Journal*, 24 (1999), pp. 68–84.

——, ' "The Faith Society"? Quantifying Religious Belonging in Edwardian Britain, 1901–1914', *Journal of Religious History*, 37 (2013), pp. 39–63.

——, 'Gradualist or Revolutionary Secularization? A Case Study of Religious Belonging in Inter-War Britain, 1918–1939', *Church History and Religious Culture*, 93 (2013), pp. 57–93.

——, 'Is the Bible Becoming a Closed Book? British Opinion Poll Evidence', *Journal of Contemporary Religion*, 29 (2014), pp. 503–28.

——, 'John Bull's Judeophobia: Images of the Jews in British Public Opinion Polls since the Late 1930s', *Jahrbuch für Antisemitismusforschung*, 15 (2006), pp. 259–300.

——, 'Joining and Leaving British Methodism since the 1960s', in L.J. Francis and Y. Katz, eds, *Joining and Leaving Religion: Research Perspectives* (Leominster: Gracewing, 2000), pp. 57–85.

——, 'Keeping the Spiritual Home Fires Burning: Religious Belonging in Britain During the First World War', *War & Society*, 33 (2014), pp. 244–68.

——, 'Long-Living Methodists', *British Religion in Numbers*, 24 June 2010, http://www.brin.ac.uk/news/2010/long-living-methodists/.

——, 'Measuring Religious Affiliation in Great Britain: The 2011 Census in Historical and Methodological Context', *Religion*, 44 (2014), pp. 357–82.

——, 'Non-Recurrent Christian Data', in W.F. Maunder, ed., *Religion* (Reviews of United Kingdom Statistical Sources, 20, Oxford: Pergamon Press, 1987), pp. 189–504.

——, 'No Popery's Ghost: Does Popular Anti-Catholicism Survive in Contemporary Britain?', *Journal of Religion in Europe*, 7 (2014), pp. 116–49.

DOI: 10.1057/9781137512536.0011

——, '*Puzzled People* Revisited: Religious Believing and Belonging in Wartime Britain, 1939–45', *Twentieth Century British History*, 19 (2008), pp. 446–79.

——, ' "A Quaint and Dangerous Anachronism"? Who Supports the (Dis)establishment of the Church of England?', *Implicit Religion*, 14 (2011), pp. 319–41.

——, *Religious Statistics in Great Britain: An Historical Introduction* (Manchester: Institute for Social Change, University of Manchester, 2010), http://www.brin.ac.uk/wp-content/uploads/2011/12/development-of-religious-statistics.pdf.

——, 'Repurposing Religious Surveys', in L. Woodhead, ed., *How to Research Religion: Putting Methods into Practice* (Oxford: Oxford University Press, forthcoming).

——, ' "The Secularised Sabbath" Revisited: Opinion Polls as Sources for Sunday Observance in Contemporary Britain', *Contemporary British History*, 15 (2001), pp. 1–20.

——, 'Zion's People: Who Were the English Nonconformists? Part 1: Gender, Age, Marital Status, and Ethnicity', *Local Historian*, 40 (2010), pp. 91–112.

Freathy, R. and Parker, S.G., 'Secularists, Humanists, and Religious Education: Religious Crisis and Curriculum Change in England, 1963–1975', *History of Education*, 42 (2013), pp. 222–56.

Freeman, M., ' "Britain's Spiritual Life: How Can It Be Deepened?" Seebohm Rowntree, Russell Lavers, and the "Crisis of Belief", ca. 1946–54', *Journal of Religious History*, 29 (2005), pp. 25–42.

Frost, B., *Goodwill on Fire: Donald Soper's Life and Mission* (London: Hodder and Stoughton, 1996).

Gallup, G.H., ed., *The Gallup International Public Opinion Polls: Great Britain, 1937–1975* (2 vols, New York: Random House, 1976).

Garnett, J., Grimley, M., Harris, A., Whyte, W., and Williams, S.C., eds, *Redefining Christian Britain: Post-1945 Perspectives* (London: SCM Press, 2006).

Gilbert, A.D., *The Making of Post-Christian Britain: A History of the Secularization of Modern Society* (London: Longman, 1980).

Gill, R., *The 'Empty' Church Revisited* (Aldershot: Ashgate, 2003).

Gill, R., Hadaway, C.K., and Marler, P.L., 'Is Religious Belief Declining in Britain?' *Journal for the Scientific Study of Religion*, 37 (1998), pp. 507–16.

DOI: 10.1057/9781137512536.0011

Gilliat-Ray, S., *Muslims in Britain: An Introduction* (Cambridge: Cambridge University Press, 2010).

Goodhew, D., 'Church Growth in Britain', *Journal of Religion in Europe*, 6 (2013), pp. 297–315.

——, ed., *Church Growth in Britain, 1980 to the Present* (Farnham: Ashgate, 2012).

Gowland, D. and Roebuck, S., *Never Call Retreat: A Biography of Bill Gowland* (London: Chester House, 1990).

Green, S.J.D., *The Passing of Protestant England: Secularisation and Social Change, c. 1920–1960* (Cambridge: Cambridge University Press, 2011).

——, 'A People beyond the Book? Seebohm Rowntree, the Decline of Popular Biblicism, and the Fate of Protestant England, c. 1900–50', in S. Mandelbrote and M. Ledger-Lomas, eds, *Dissent and the Bible in Britain, c. 1650–1950* (Oxford: Oxford University Press, 2013), pp. 256–76.

——, 'Social Science and the Discovery of a "Post-Protestant People"', *Northern History*, 45 (2008), pp. 87–109.

——, 'Was There an English Religious Revival in the 1950s?', *Journal of the United Reformed Church History Society*, 7 (2006), pp. 517–38.

Grimley, M., 'The Religion of Englishness: Puritanism, Providentialism, and "National Character", 1918–1945', *Journal of British Studies*, 46 (2007), pp. 884–906.

Hagerty, J., 'The Conversion of England: John Carmel Heenan and the Catholic Missionary Society, 1947–1951', *Recusant History*, 31 (2013), pp. 461–81.

Halsey, A.H. and Webb, J., eds, *Twentieth-Century British Social Trends* (Basingstoke: Macmillan, 2000).

Harris, A. and Spence, M., ' "Disturbing the Complacency of Religion"? The Evangelical Crusades of Dr Billy Graham and Father Patrick Peyton in Britain, 1951–54', *Twentieth Century British History*, 18 (2007), pp. 481–513.

Hastings, A., *A History of English Christianity, 1920–1985* (London: Collins, 1986).

Hennessy, P., *Never Again: Britain, 1945–51* (London: Jonathan Cape, 1992).

Hinton, J., *The Mass Observers: A History, 1937–1949* (Oxford: Oxford University Press, 2013).

Houlbrooke, M., *Rite Out of Time: A Study of the Ancient Rite of Churching and its Survival in the Twentieth Century* (Donington: Shaun Tyas, 2011).

DOI: 10.1057/9781137512536.0011

James, A.J. and Thomas, J.E., *Wales at Westminster: A History of the Parliamentary Representation of Wales, 1800–1979* (Llandysul: Gomer Press, 1981).

Jeremy, D.J., *Capitalists and Christians: Business Leaders and the Churches in Britain, 1900–1960* (Oxford: Clarendon Press, 1990).

Jones, B.E., *Family Count: A Study Pamphlet about Methodism Today* (London: Methodist Church Home Mission Department, 1970).

Jones, I., *The Local Church and Generational Change in Birmingham, 1945–2000* (Woodbridge: Boydell Press, 2012).

Kay, W.K., 'Belief in God in Great Britain, 1945–1996: Moving the Scenery Behind Classroom RE', *British Journal of Religious Education*, 20 (1997-98), pp. 28–41.

Kirby, D., *Church, State, and Propaganda: The Archbishop of York and International Relations – A Political Study of Cyril Foster Garbett, 1942–1955* (Hull: University of Hull Press, 1999).

——, ed., *Religion and the Cold War* (Basingstoke: Palgrave Macmillan, 2003).

Kushner, T., *We Europeans? Mass-Observation, 'Race', and British Identity in the Twentieth Century* (Aldershot: Ashgate, 2004).

Kynaston, D., *Family Britain, 1951–57* (London: Bloomsbury, 2009).

Legerton, H.J.W., *For Our Lord and His Day: A History of the Lord's Day Observance Society* (Leicester: printed by Oldham & Manton, [?1993]).

Machin, G.I.T., 'British Churches and Social Issues, 1945–60', *Twentieth Century British History*, 7 (1996), pp. 345–70.

——, *Churches and Social Issues in Twentieth-Century Britain* (Oxford: Clarendon Press, 1998).

Maiden, J. and Webster, P., 'Parliament, the Church of England, and the Last Gasp of Political Protestantism, 1963–4', *Parliamentary History*, 32 (2013), pp. 361–77.

Martin, D.A., *The Education of David Martin: The Making of an Unlikely Sociologist* (London: SPCK, 2013).

Marwick, A., *The Sixties: Cultural Revolution in Britain, France, Italy, and the United States, c. 1958–c. 1974* (Oxford: Oxford University Press, 1998).

McLeod, H., 'The 1960s', in I. Katznelson and G. Stedman Jones, eds, *Religion and the Political Imagination* (Cambridge: Cambridge University Press, 2010), pp. 254–74.

——, 'The Crisis of Christianity in the West: Entering a Post-Christian Era?', in H. McLeod, ed., *The Cambridge History of Christianity,*

DOI: 10.1057/9781137512536.0011

Volume 9: World Christianities, c. 1914–c. 2000 (Cambridge: Cambridge University Press, 2006), pp. 323–47.

——, 'European Religion in the 1960s', in S. Hermle, C. Lepp, and H. Oelke, eds, *Umbrüche: der deutsche Protestantismus und die sozialen Bewegungen in den 1960er und 70er Jahren* (2nd edn, Göttingen: Vandenhoeck & Ruprecht, 2012), pp. 35–50.

——, 'God and the Gallows: Christianity and Capital Punishment in the Nineteenth and Twentieth Centuries', in K. Cooper and J. Gregory, eds, *Retribution, Repentance, and Reconciliation* (*Studies in Church History*, 40, Woodbridge: Boydell Press, 2004), pp. 330–56.

——, 'The Religious Crisis of the 1960s', *Journal of Modern European History*, 3 (2005), pp. 205–30.

——, *The Religious Crisis of the 1960s* (Oxford: Oxford University Press, 2007).

——, 'The Sixties: Writing the Religious History of a Critical Decade', *Kirchliche Zeitgeschichte*, 14 (2001), pp. 36–48.

——, 'Why Were the 1960s So Religiously Explosive?', *Nederlands Theologisch Tijdschrift*, 60 (2006), pp. 109–30.

Merritt, R.L. and Puchala, D.J., eds, *Western European Perspectives on International Affairs: Public Opinion Studies and Evaluations* (New York: Frederick A. Praeger, 1968).

Miller, W.L. and Raab, G., 'The Religious Alignment at English Elections between 1918 and 1970', *Political Studies*, 25 (1977), pp. 227–51.

Moon, N., *Opinion Polls: History, Theory, and Practice* (Manchester: Manchester University Press, 1999).

Morgan, D.D., *The Span of the Cross: Christian Religion and Society in Wales, 1914–2000* (Cardiff: University of Wales Press, 1999).

Morris, J., '*Church and People* Thirty-Three Years On: A Historical Critique', *Theology*, 94 (1991), pp. 92–101.

Parker, S.G., *Faith on the Home Front: Aspects of Church Life and Popular Religion in Birmingham, 1939–1945* (Oxford: Peter Lang, 2005).

Parsons, G., 'How the Times They Were a-Changing: Exploring the Context of Religious Transformation in Britain in the 1960s', in J.R. Wolffe, ed., *Religion in History: Conflict, Conversion, and Coexistence* (Manchester: Open University Press, 2004), pp. 161–89.

Peach, C. and Gale, R., 'Muslims, Hindus, and Sikhs in the New Religious Landscape of England', *Geographical Review*, 93 (2003), pp. 469–90.

Pickering, W.S.F., 'The Persistence of Rites of Passage: Towards an Explanation', *British Journal of Sociology*, 25 (1974), pp. 63–78.

DOI: 10.1057/9781137512536.0011

——, 'The Secularized Sabbath: Formerly Sunday, Now the Weekend', in M. Hill, ed., *A Sociological Yearbook of Religion in Britain, 5* (London: SCM Press, 1972), pp. 33–47.

——, 'Who Goes to Church?', in C.L. Mitton, ed., *The Social Sciences and the Churches* (Edinburgh: T. & T. Clark, 1972), pp. 181–97.

Potter [née Taylor], C.R., 'Is Home Where the Heart Is? Jamaican Migration and British Churches, 1948–1965', *Wesley Historical Society of London and the South East Journal*, 80 (2011), pp. 4–13.

Potter, H., *Hanging in Judgment: Religion and the Death Penalty in England from the Bloody Code to Abolition* (London: SCM Press, 1993).

Randall, I.M., 'Billy Graham, Evangelism, and Fundamentalism', in D.W. Bebbington and D.C. Jones, eds, *Evangelicalism and Fundamentalism in the United Kingdom During the Twentieth Century* (Oxford: Oxford University Press, 2013), pp. 173–91.

——, 'Conservative Constructionist: The Early Influence of Billy Graham in Britain', *Evangelical Quarterly*, 67 (1995), pp. 309–33.

——, *The English Baptists of the Twentieth Century* (Didcot: Baptist Historical Society, 2005).

Randall, I.M. and Hilborn, D., *One Body in Christ: The History and Significance of the Evangelical Alliance* (Carlisle: Paternoster Press, 2001).

Roberts, E., 'The Lancashire Way of Death', in R. Houlbrooke, ed., *Death, Ritual, and Bereavement* (London: Routledge, 1989), pp. 188–207.

Roodhouse, M., ' "Fish-and-Chip Intelligence": Henry Durant and the British Institute of Public Opinion, 1936–63', *Twentieth Century British History*, 24 (2013), pp. 224–48.

Rosman, D., 'Sunday Schools and Social Change in the Twentieth Century', in S. Orchard and J.H.Y. Briggs, eds, *The Sunday School Movement: Studies in the Growth and Decline of Sunday Schools* (Milton Keynes: Paternoster, 2007), pp. 149–60.

Sendall, B., Potter, J., and Bonner, P., *Independent Television in Britain* (6 vols, London: Macmillan, 1982–2003).

Singh, G. and Tatla, D.S., *Sikhs in Britain: The Making of a Community* (London: Zed Books, 2006).

Spencer, A.E.C.W., 'Alienation in English Catholicism, 1958–1972', in A.E.C.W. Spencer and P.A. O'Dwyer, eds, *Proceedings of the Second Annual Conference, Sociological Association of Ireland, Dublin, 4–5 April 1975* (Belfast: Department of Social Studies, Queen's University of Belfast, 1976), pp. 115–34.

DOI: 10.1057/9781137512536.0011

——, ed., *Annotated Bibliography of Newman Demographic Survey Reports & Papers, 1954–1964* (Taunton: Russell-Spencer, 2006).

——, 'Catholics in Britain and Ireland: Regional Contrasts', in D.A. Coleman, ed., *Demography of Immigrants and Minority Groups in the United Kingdom* (London: Academic Press, 1982), pp. 213–43.

——, 'Demography of Catholicism', *The Month*, 2nd New Series, 8 (1975), pp. 100–5.

——, ed., *Digest of Statistics of the Catholic Community of England & Wales, 1958–2005, Volume 1: Population and Vital Statistics, Pastoral Services, Evangelisation, and Education* (Taunton: Russell-Spencer, 2007).

——, 'The Newman Demographic Survey', in *A Use of Gifts: The Newman Association, 1942–1992* (London: Newman Association, 1992), pp. 34–7.

——, *Services for Catholic Migrants, 1939–2008: Background Data from the Archives and Databank of the Newman Demographic Survey and the Pastoral Research Centre* (Taunton: Russell-Spencer, 2008).

Stanton, N., 'From Sunday Schools to Christian Youth Work: Young People's Engagement with Organised Christianity in Twentieth Century England and the Present Day' (PhD thesis, Open University, 2013).

Sykes, R.P.M., 'Popular Religion in Decline: A Study from the Black Country', *Journal of Ecclesiastical History*, 56 (2005), pp. 287–307.

——, 'Popular Religion in Dudley and the Gornals, *c.* 1914–1965' (PhD thesis, University of Wolverhampton, 1999).

Taylor, C.R., 'British Churches and Jamaican Migration: A Study of Religion and Identities, 1948 to 1965' (PhD thesis, Anglia Polytechnic University, 2002).

Thompson, D., *Donald Soper: A Biography* (Nutfield: Denholm House Press, 1971).

Thompson, D.M., *The Decline of Congregationalism in the Twentieth Century* (London: Congregational Memorial Hall Trust, 2002).

Trzebiatowska, M. and Bruce, S., *Why Are Women More Religious Than Men?* (Oxford: Oxford University Press, 2012).

Twitchell, N., *The Politics of the Rope: The Campaign to Abolish Capital Punishment in Britain, 1955–1969* (Bury St Edmunds: Arena, 2012).

Voas, D., 'Intermarriage and the Demography of Secularization', *British Journal of Sociology*, 54 (2003), pp. 83–108.

Wadsworth, M.E.J. and Freeman, S.R., 'Generation Differences in Beliefs: A Cohort Study of Stability and Change in Religious Beliefs', *British Journal of Sociology*, 34 (1983), pp. 416–37.

DOI: 10.1057/9781137512536.0011

Wigley, J., *The Rise and Fall of the Victorian Sunday* (Manchester: Manchester University Press, 1980).

Williams, J., *Digest of Welsh Historical Statistics* (2 vols, Cardiff: Welsh Office, 1985).

Williams, S.C., *Religious Belief and Popular Culture in Southwark, c. 1880–1939* (Oxford: Oxford University Press, 1999).

——, 'Urban Popular Religion and the Rites of Passage', in H. McLeod, ed., *European Religion in the Age of Great Cities, 1830–1930* (London: Routledge, 1995), pp. 216–36.

Williamson, P., 'National Days of Prayer: The Churches, the State, and Public Worship in Britain, 1899–1957', *English Historical Review*, 128 (2013), pp. 323–66.

Wilson, C.M., 'The Sunday Opening Referenda, 1961–1989: A Study in Social and Cultural Change in Wales' (MPhil thesis, University of Wales, Aberystwyth, 1993).

Wolfe, J.N. and Pickford, M., *The Church of Scotland: An Economic Survey* (London: Geoffrey Chapman, 1980).

Wolfe, K.M., *The Churches and the British Broadcasting Corporation, 1922–1956: The Politics of Broadcast Religion* (London: SCM Press, 1984).

Wolffe, J.R., 'Change and Continuity in British Anti-Catholicism, 1829–1982', in F. Tallett and N. Atkin, eds, *Catholicism in Britain and France since 1789* (London: Hambledon Press, 1996), pp. 67–83.

Wright, S., *The Sounds of the Sixties and the Church* (Guildford: Grosvenor House, 2008).

Wybrow, R.J., *Britain Speaks Out, 1937–87: A Social History as Seen Through the Gallup Data* (Basingstoke: Macmillan, 1989).

Yalden, P.J., 'Association, Community, and the Origins of Secularisation: English and Welsh Nonconformity, c. 1850–1930', *Journal of Ecclesiastical History*, 55 (2004), pp. 293–324.

Yates, N., *Love Now, Pay Later? Sex and Religion in the Fifties and Sixties* (London: SPCK, 2010).

Ziegler, P., *Crown and People* (London: Collins, 1978).

DOI: 10.1057/9781137512536.0011

Index

The table of contents is intended to be the principal means of navigating this short book. This index is confined to specific religious groups, persons, places, and topics which are discussed in the text (excluding the preliminary pages) or, in a few instances, expanded on in an endnote. In order to maintain focus, it does not attempt to reference bibliographical details (of authors, titles, and subjects) of primary and secondary sources which are recorded in table source notes, endnotes, and bibliography.

DOI: 10.1057/9781137512536.0012

DOI: 10.1057/9781137512536.0012

DOI: 10.1057/9781137512536.0012

DOI: 10.1057/9781137512536.0012

DOI: 10.1057/9781137512536.0012

CPSIA information can be obtained at www.ICGtesting.com
Printed in the USA
LVOW11*1837050615

441371LV00003B/24/P